I0447560

A Policymaker's Guide to Bioterrorism and What to Do About It

By Richard J. Danzig

Center for Technology and National Security Policy
National Defense University
December 2009

Contents

Introduction

The terrorist attacks of September 11, 2001, brought together two related but distinct phenomena. First, they presented the calling card of al Qaeda and more generally of militant Islam. These attacks were rightly perceived as an act of war by a group seeking to catalyze a political-religious movement. Much of America's effort since then has been to destroy that group, its sanctuaries, and its affiliates; some of the effort has been to counter the psychological, social, and political appeal of militant (predominantly Wahabi) Islam.

Second, these attacks introduced the public to a more general phenomenon: our vulnerability to acts of terror on a greater scale than anything America had experienced. It is remarkable that in the turbulent 20th century, which witnessed some 200 million deaths from politically driven violence and war, no single attack on American soil equaled the estimated 3,000 deaths on 9/11.[1] The implications for America are the graver because the capability to inflict carnage at this level—and at much higher levels—is not confined to a group or movement. It lies at hand as an instrument that can be used by any belligerent group (or state, or individual). It will survive the destruction of al Qaeda and the abandonment of jihad.

These two strands—jihadi terrorism and our general vulnerability to terror on a large scale—intertwine but are independent.[2] The tendency to confuse them is accentuated when policymakers rhetorically jump from one to the other; the effect resembles one produced by the thaumatrope, a popular 19th-century toy now encountered only as a curiosity.[3] A horse is depicted on one side of a disk or card and a man on the other, or a cage on one side and a bird on the other. When the object is spun quickly, the rider appears on the horse, or the bird in the cage. Our inability to separate images shown us in rapid succession merges the two in our minds.

We speak of a "war on terror" (not just on al Qaeda) and have devoted significant resources to controlling and preparing for the consequences of "weapons of mass destruction," but these efforts overwhelmingly focus on the present challenge of jihadi fundamentalism. Our inherent vulnerability to large-scale terrorism is more troubling but less addressed.

Starkly contrasting statements made by President George W. Bush half a day apart indicate the difficulty of disentangling the two strands. On the *Today Show* on August 30, 2004, President Bush was asked when the war on terror would end. His answer was that it had no end. The next

---

[1] The Japanese attack on Pearl Harbor produced 2,403 deaths. In the 19th century, some Civil War battles exceeded 50,000 deaths. See <www.civilwarhome.com/Battles.htm>.

[2] For the most prominent statement, see President George W. Bush: "The gravest danger to freedom lies at the perilous crossroads of radicalism and technology. When the spread of chemical and biological and nuclear weapons, along with ballistic missile technology — when that occurs, even weak states and small groups could attain a catastrophic power to strike great nations." See "Remarks at the Graduation Exercise of the United States Military Academy," June 1, 2002, available at <www.whitehouse.gov/news/releases/2002/06/20020601-3.html>.

[3] I am indebted to the late Leon Lipson for this metaphor.

morning, responding to a political uproar, the President told the American Legion that the war could and would be won. The second statement is correct if we think of this as a war on al Qaeda or against militant jihadis. The first statement is correct if we think of this as a war against terror because neither the instrument of terror nor our vulnerability to terrorism can be eradicated. Confusion arises from the application of the same term to two different phenomena, *threats* and *risks*.

A sounder approach would rigorously distinguish between the two strands. Al Qaeda and its allies and affiliates are a *threat*. Particular terrorist groups like these can (and probably will) be eradicated. Though the manner and time of a resolution with groups like the Taliban in Afghanistan and Pakistan, Hamas in Gaza, Hezbollah in Lebanon, and other diverse entities cannot be predicted, history shows that a resolution—violent or pacific or both—is likely to come.[4]

Our vulnerability to the use of chemical, biological, radiological, nuclear, and other technologies to create terror is a *risk*. These technologies provide instruments that can be seized upon by any group for use as weapons of terror. So long as grievances exist and those who hold grievances are willing to resort to violence, the use of such weapons will be an enduring risk. The sweep of history suggests that these risks cannot be eradicated. Apart from the dum-dum bullet, we cannot point to examples of effective weapons that have not been used. Once used successfully, weapons tend to proliferate. That proliferation is abetted when the skills that can produce a weapon are closely related to civilian skills and equipment that are themselves proliferating. To cope with our inherent vulnerability to weapons of terror, we must find strategies of risk management.

There is an important difference in the time dimensions in which we should think about the two strands. For more than a decade, al Qaeda, for example, has been a clear and present danger. Our broader and more enduring risks from bioterrorism are neither so clear nor so evidently immediate. In contrast to al Qaeda, however, they are predictably more dangerous in the future than in the present.

The concept of a war on terror is misleading when applied to the second strand of enduring risks. A war is a state of emergency in which an opponent is defined and tactical initiatives are imperative. In wars we have known (consider, for example, World Wars I and II, Korea, and Vietnam), "strategies" have been plans for the current year, the next one, and maybe the year after. A long-term risk requires research and development of technologies, social approaches, and long-term intelligence training, manpower, and deployment investments against a range of now unidentified, and indeed, in some respects, unpredictable opponents.

It was sometimes said about our experience in Vietnam that, though we fought for a decade, we conducted not a single 10-year war, but ten 1-year wars. We must avoid replicating this failure in defending against the new means of terrorism by reacting to the "threat du jour."

---

[4] A recent RAND Corporation study examined 648 terror groups that existed between 1968 and 2006. The authors observed that, of those groups, "244 are alive and 136 splintered (thereby ending the group but not ending the terrorism), leaving 268 that came to an end in ways that eliminated their contribution to terrorism." See Seth G. Jones and Martin C. Libicki, *How Terrorist Groups End: Lessons for Countering al Qa'ida* (Santa Monica, CA: RAND, 2008), 35. According to the study, "Terrorist groups end for two major reasons: Members decide to adopt non-violent tactics and join the political process (43 percent), or local law enforcement agencies arrest or kill members of the group (40 percent). Military force has rarely been the primary reason for the end of terrorist groups (7 percent), and few groups since 1968 have achieved victory (10 percent)," 18–19.

If we accept that our risk from the proliferation of the many means of terrorism is broad and enduring, then we need a strategy with a long time horizon that addresses many risks.

Devising such a strategy would be difficult for leaders at any time and place, but it is particularly challenging for leaders focused on what they regard as imperative, near-term threats, and for complex, divided, democratic societies with pressing priorities and problems. Moreover, members of our impressively professional security establishment are trained and rewarded in ways that undervalue addressing long-term risks. Promotion and recognition are awarded for achievement in the short term. Most fundamentally, professional systems generally facilitate skills and empower agendas relevant to familiar past problems, not potential future ones. These traits pose challenges for reformers who want to address new risks. They must fight for new analyses, modernized security systems, reorganization to achieve a fresh focus, and new measures of progress. However challenging this effort, jihadi groups can be pursued with familiar instruments and through established organizations (particularly the Department of Defense [DOD] and intelligence agencies). Applying well-developed, professional skills in a new context, our national security establishment is moving toward a consensus view of the enemy, broadly useful models of how it is financed, organized, recruits, trains, and plans, and a set of theories about how to counter these activities over the next few years.[5]

The enduring risks, by contrast, demand original thinking, rather as nuclear weapons and the communist threat demanded and elicited new paradigms in the decade after World War II. What is required is often uncomfortable because it is not the incremental adjustment of old organizations and the adaptation of established professional skills. The requirement is radical rather than reformist. It is disruptive in its demands for debate about accepted premises and its claim for resources that probably will be diverted from longstanding priorities. It is not surprising that the debate is underdeveloped and that we do not have the necessary body of new thinking.

This paper draws together several years of work in an attempt to suggest the outlines of this thinking about the risk that I regard as most pernicious: biological terrorism. It is written for those who desire a better understanding of this risk and its implications for policymakers.

---

[5] An early description may be found in *The 9/11 Commission Report: Final Report of the National Commission on Terrorist Attacks Upon the United States* (Washington, DC: Government Printing Office, 2004), 169–173. There are, of course, differences in view still being debated. Compare, for example, Marc Sageman, *Understanding Terror Networks* (Philadelphia: University of Pennsylvania Press, 2004), setting forth essentially a secular view of recruitment by establishing social alternatives to alienation, with Stephen P. Lambert, *Y: The Sources of Islamic Revolutionary Conduct* (Washington, DC: Center for Strategic Intelligence Research, Joint Military Intelligence College, 2005), ascribing recruitment dominantly to religious motivations. See also the more recent debate between Sageman and Bruce Hoffman of the RAND Corporation as reflected in Bruce Hoffman, "The Myth of Grass Roots Terrorism: Why Osama Bin Laden Still Matters," *Foreign Affairs* (May/June, 2008), which reviews Sageman's book *Leaderless Jihad: Terror Networks in the Twenty-First Century* (Philadelphia: University of Pennsylvania Press, 2008): "Sageman's impressive résumé cannot overcome his fundamental misreading of the al Qaeda threat." Sageman and Hoffman continue their debate under the heading, "Does Osama Still Call the Shots: Debating the Containment of al-Qaeda's Leadership," Foreign Affairs (July/August 2008).

Section I delineates the problem that confronts us. It describes the character and magnitude of the risk of biological terrorism and identifies the factors that differentiate bioterrorism from other modes of terrorism. This section also comments on why biological terrorism has not yet emerged as an important instrument of terror and offers judgments about the likelihood of its manifestation over the next decade.

Section II enumerates four factors that have confused, confounded, and constrained the U.S. response to this threat.

Section III, the most operational part of this paper, offers my top 10 recommendations for moving ahead.

I. The Nature and Probability of Bioterrorism

Appreciating the Unique Attributes of Bioterrorism

The phrase *weapons of mass destruction* (WMD) is embedded in our present jargon. Bioterrorism is widely accepted as a central example of WMD. Indeed, at the turn of the century, WMD was considered synonymous with *NBC*—nuclear,[6] biological, and chemical weapons. Subsequently, the term was expanded to include radiological weapons (so-called dirty bombs, made by pairing conventional explosive weaponry with radioactive material),[7] and then sometimes expanded further to include conventional explosive weapons that could produce large effects, yielding the frequently encountered initialism *CBRNE* (chemical, biological, radiological, nuclear, and high-yield explosive). Most recently, concern regarding CBRNE has been supplemented by recognition of cyber risks arising from our governmental and private sector reliance on computers and their vulnerability to software and hardware intrusion and manipulation. How does bioterrorism fit into this WMD mélange?

Biological terrorism involves the use of pathogens—bacteria, viruses, and toxins produced by living things—as a means of attacking civilian populations. The methods by which these pathogens might be dispersed are diverse. They include employing aerosol sprayers, contaminating food or drink (including water supplies), and using people or animals as vectors by infecting them with contagious pathogens. Attacks may aim at killing people, burdening our health care and protective systems, decimating agricultural and animal industries,[8] contaminating equipment, facilities, or areas, or simply distracting our government's energies and causing confusion, hysteria, and perhaps panic.

An aerosol attack using a kilogram of anthrax (bacteria that would be inhaled) configured to disperse fairly efficiently, or an attack that introduced smallpox (a contagious virus) into our presently unvaccinated population could reasonably be expected to kill tens of thousands of people. It could take decades after an anthrax attack before Manhattan could be restored to the point where deaths were not caused by residual contamination. A communicable disease like smallpox would

---

[6] For a skeptical look at possible terrorist use of nuclear weapons, see Brian Jenkins, *Will Terrorists Go Nuclear?* (Amherst, NY: Prometheus Books, 2008).

[7] For an attempt to quantify this risk, see Heather Rosoff and Detlof von Winterfeldt, "A Risk and Economic Analysis of Dirty Bomb Attacks on the Ports of Los Angeles and Long Beach," *Risk Analysis*, vol. 27 (2007), 533ff. After assessing a range of dirty bomb scenarios as though they were business projects (the authors used Microsoft Project software), the authors judged that in the median case attackers would have a 20 to 40 percent probability of success. (538–539).

[8] Foot and mouth disease—a virus common among animal populations in the developing world, but not present in the United States for over 75 years—would affect only our population of pigs, poultry, and cattle, but if introduced among them would likely cause over $10 billion of damage, and its containment would require substantial travel restrictions and animal killings.

have smaller enduring effects from contamination, but could kill more people and inspire more fear, with consequent collateral effects on our economy and our society.

These facts put biological weaponry on the same plane as nuclear weapons; they can be catastrophic, whether measured by deaths and injuries or economic, operational, or psychological effects. Conventional explosives, radiation-enhanced conventional explosives, chemical attacks, and cyber attacks all can do great damage, but they do not have such broad-scale potential. Without belaboring the point, it is appropriate to observe that biological and nuclear attacks can be an order of magnitude more consequential than attacks employing other weaponry.

Unfortunately, the linkage of nuclear and biological weapons is also misleading. The well-developed thinking about how to cope with nuclear weapons provides a poor model for thinking about bioterrorism. It is important to appreciate a half-dozen characteristics that distinguish biological from nuclear weapons.

1. Pathogenic material and equipment for amplifying pathogens is much more readily obtainable than nuclear material.

Nuclear proliferation can be prevented by controlling four items or activities:

- fissile materials (plutonium and highly enriched uranium)
- the activities and equipment (principally centrifuges) that extract plutonium from spent reactor fuel or convert uranium (which is common) into fissile material (which is scarce and closely monitored)
- warheads that have been fabricated from plutonium or highly enriched uranium
- testing of nuclear weapons.

International efforts to control these activities, material, and equipment have been imperfect, but still impressive in their success. On the one hand, the number of nuclear states has grown from 5 to 9,[9] Iran is threatening to become a tenth, and experts have warned of the risk of terrorists seizing or buying nuclear weapons. On the other hand, the number of states that have achieved nuclear status has been constrained, and no nuclear weapons have been identified in terrorists' hands.

Moreover, even with the failures of our nuclear control regime, it is widely believed that it is possible to control the items on this list. As a result, we have a theory of nuclear nonproliferation and a large international effort that—imperfectly but substantially—puts that theory into practice. By contrast, we have effective means of controlling only a small fraction of biological material, equipment, test, and experimentation.

---

[9] The original five nuclear weapon states (the United States, Russia, United Kingdom, France, and China) have apparently been joined by Israel, India, Pakistan, and North Korea. South Africa, which may have conducted a nuclear test, dismantled its nuclear weapon program.

As a result, though most nations subscribe to the principle that biological weapons should be controlled,[10] we have no strategy, much less a comprehensive practice, to prevent biological arms proliferation, or even to slow it appreciably.

There are three paths to obtaining a pathogen: harvest it from nature, obtain it from a research center, or create it by either modifying another pathogen or synthesizing it from its obtainable components.

Harvesting. Over 1,000 pathogens that exist in nature are inimical to man. Many of these can be harvested from the soil, air, or the bodies of infected animals or people. Scores of these can be cultured using well-established methods. It is as though enriched uranium could be distilled from soil, or as though we were attempting gun control when guns grew on trees.

Ordering. Culture libraries have also made pathogens more easily accessible. Controls on access to particularly virulent pathogens tightened in the United States and abroad after the 2001 anthrax letter attacks, but these controls vary between nations,[11] and a large number of samples have already been dispersed. Research on vaccines and drugs, combined with requirements for education and training, have resulted in tens of thousands of pathogens being present in laboratories throughout the world.[12]

Creating. The new biology has facilitated the creation of viruses and bacteria from material that can be transferred from other organisms or be synthesized from snippets purchased from commercial providers.[13]

---

[10] The two major international commitments in this regard are the Biological and Toxic Weapons Convention and United Nations (UN) Security Council Resolution 1540. The former, forswearing state biological offensive weapons programs, is codified in UN General Assembly Resolution 2826 (XXVI), 1972: "Convention on the Prohibition of the Development, Production and Stockpiling of Bacteriological (Biological) and Toxin Weapons and on Their Destruction." The latter provides an important 21st-century expansion (it was passed in 2004) by focusing on prohibiting state support to nonstate actors seeking weapons of mass destruction (WMD). Resolution 1540 led the creation of a three member International Support Unit that is doing useful work identifying national efforts to control pathogens, comparing different approaches, and providing training. See generally the U.S. Statement Department Web site comments supporting Resolution 1540 at <www.state.gov/t/isn/c18943.htm>, and UN Security Council, "Report of the Committee established pursuant to Security Council resolution 1540 (2004)," July 30, 2008.

[11] "38 States reported having measures in place to account for biological weapon-related materials, whereas 53 States reported having measures in place to secure them. While this may indicate an increased awareness by States of the potential risk from the accidental release of biological weapon-related materials, the Committee notes that only 25 States reported having measures in place to undertake reliability checks of personnel working with sensitive materials." See UN Security Council, "Report of the Committee established pursuant to Security Council resolution 1540 (2004)," July 30, 2008, 13. The 1540 committee also reports that 71 states reported having licensing provisions for "biological weapon-related material" (15).

[12] The United States alone has almost 1,400 high containment biosafety laboratories (BSL–3 and BSL–4), each of which may contain many strains of pathogen. See U.S. Government Accountability Office (GAO), *High-Containment Biosafety Laboratories: Preliminary Observations on the Oversight of the Proliferation of BSL–3 and BSL–4 Laboratories in the United States*, GAO-08-108T (Washington, DC: GAO, 2007), 10, available at <www.gao.gov/new.items/d08108t.pdf>.

[13] The accessibility of these technologies is suggested by articles such as Marcus Wilson, "Do It Yourself Genetic Engineering," available at <www.nbcbayarea.com/health/tips_info/NATL-Do-It-Yourself-Gene.html>. The article ends with a comment by one home genetic engineer that to master the relevant skills: a "terrorist doesn't need [special sources for equipment and knowledge]. [He] can just enroll in [his] local community college."

Thus, while nuclear proliferation can be controlled by controlling the production and distribution of plutonium and highly enriched uranium, bioterrorism can only be damped, not controlled, by restricting material.

2. Supplies of pathogenic material are much more easily increased than are supplies of nuclear material.

In a conducive environment, pathogens reproduce. In such an environment, anthrax bacteria double their population every 20 to 30 minutes. In a day, a properly supported population will grow a billion-fold at the low end. Some bacteria and viruses are more difficult to grow than others, but the science and art of fermentation are well documented and are facilitated by ever-improving technologies.

As a result, the nuclear and biological threats are fundamentally different. The nuclear threat arises from the risk of theft or illegal seizure or purchase of nuclear material that can be *fabricated* into one or a few weapons. The biological threat is that terrorists will obtain the skills and materials for *producing* weapons. Once obtained, these skills and materials can all too easily be disseminated.

3. The recent revolution in biotechnology has proliferated, and predictably will continue to proliferate knowledge, skills, and equipment that can be applied to develop and use biological weapons.

Just as the invention of the semiconductor at midcentury enabled an information revolution over the last quarter of the 20th century, so have advances in biotechnology in recent decades initiated a revolution in biological sciences. An observation made by a task force of the Defense Science Board 7 years ago is even more emphatically the case today:

> There is no area of science that is developing more rapidly than modern biology, and no area of technology developing more rapidly than modern medicine. . . . This understanding can, unfortunately, be applied, with only a modest shift of emphasis, to *causing* disease and thwarting medical treatment. . . . The *existing* capabilities in biological weapons pose a very large threat to the [United States]. . . . Advanced, optimized biological weapons could be catastrophically effective.[14]

Concepts derived from the discovery of the structure and sequencing of DNA and related genetic materials have deepened understanding and led to new technologies and techniques (particularly polymerase chain reaction and synthesis). These have been supplemented by improvements in well-established practices (for example, fermentation and the distribution of aerosols). Today, as well discerned by a National Academy of Sciences paper, biological capabilities

---

[14] "Report of the Defense Science Board/Threat Reduction Advisory Committee Task Force on Biological Defense," (Washington, DC: Office of the Under Secretary of Defense for Acquisition, Technology, and Logistics, June 2001), 11-12. For a good overview of the problem, see Ben Petro et al., "Biotechnology: Impact on Biological Warfare and Biodefense," *Biosecurity and Bioterrorism: Biodefense Strategy, Practice, and Science* 1, no. 3 (2003), 161–168.

blur "the longstanding distinction between fundamental and applied research that has served as the basis for much of at least U.S. policy toward balancing scientific openness and controls on research and dissemination in the name of security."[15] Concomitantly, there has been a worldwide distribution of biological knowledge and equipment through educational institutions (even at the high school level, but especially in college programs and graduate schools) and industries (including pharmaceuticals and biotechnology companies). As in other domains, the Internet contributes to the dissemination of knowledge and the sale and resale of equipment. In combination, these factors bring a general capability to obtain and proliferate pathogens into the hands of millions of people. As a respected scientist recently summarized the situation:

> Today, anyone with a high school education can use widely available protocols and prepackaged kits to modify the sequence of a gene or replace genes within a microorganism; one can also purchase small, disposable, self-contained bioreactors for propagating viruses and microorganisms. Such advances continue to lower the barriers to biologic-weapons development.[16]

General knowledge should not be equated with the ability to make and sustain an efficacious weapon. In some instances, practically nothing needs to be done to obtain and deploy a pathogen. The foot and mouth virus, for example, can readily be obtained from the snot or blood of an animal suffering from the disease, preserved by rudimentary techniques, and disseminated by rubbing it on the nostrils of another animal. The contagion rate is so high, and animals so frequently and variably exposed to one another, that if undetected and unchecked (difficult tasks for a defender), a few initial cases will rapidly multiply into the millions. Other viruses and bacterial strains are more difficult to obtain (for example, smallpox no longer exists naturally), require more precautions for those who would work with them, and are more difficult to amplify and sustain. Between these two poles, a bacterium like anthrax readily can be obtained in relatively benign forms, but is more difficult to obtain in a form that would be highly virulent to humans. Genetic manipulation to convert a benign strain into a more virulent strain, and then amplify a manipulated strain, can be challenging. The most effective form of dissemination, aerosol spraying, introduces some further, modest complexity.

But compared to working with nuclear materials, the challenges of developing the requisite know-how and obtaining the required equipment for bioterrorism are modest. The hurdles that

---

[15] Jo L. Husbands, "The Particular and Peculiar Case of Biotechnology," Paper presented at the annual meeting of the International Studies Association 48th Annual Convention, Chicago, IL, February 28, 2007, abstract available at <www.allacademic.com/meta/p178832_index.html>.

[16] David A. Relman, "Bioterrorism—Preparing to Fight the Next War," *The New England Journal of Medicine* 354, no. 2 (2006), 113–115. Dr. Relman's comment continued: "So far, nature has been the most effective bioterrorist. In the future, however, the ability of experimenters to create genetic or molecular diversity not found in the natural world—for example, with the use of molecular breeding technologies— and to select for virulence-associated traits may result in new biologic agents with previously unknown potency. Although such agents may not survive long in the natural world and could, from an evolutionary standpoint, be dismissed as poorly adapted competitors, they may prove extremely destructive during their lifespan."

impede obtaining an effective biological weapon will vary from pathogen to pathogen, according to the mode of distribution and the efficiency desired by an attacker. But all these hurdles are being lowered by the dissemination of knowledge, techniques, and equipment.[17]

4. There are many fewer possibilities for recognizing the production of biological weapons than for nuclear weapons—this diminishes our intelligence, law enforcement, and counterproliferation capabilities.

The envelopes mailed to the Senate in the 2001 anthrax attacks contained only about a gram of material, but each was composed of approximately a trillion spores of *b. anthracis*, the pathogen that causes anthrax. If inhaled, some 10,000 spores of virulent *b. anthracis* would typically kill a person, so a kilogram of these bacteria could theoretically kill every person on the planet. In fact, impurities, additives, and, most importantly, imperfections in distribution will render a kilogram likely to kill "only" tens of thousands of people, if effectively distributed. From this example, it will be seen that no more than small production facilities and low-visibility transport and storage mechanisms are required for effective biological terrorism.

Unfortunately for our intelligence and law enforcement agencies, these facilities have low signatures. The equipment they require—fermenters, test tubes, microscopes, freezers, dryers, and sprayers for dissemination—is commonplace in academia, the pharmaceutical and biotechnology industries, breweries, and veterinary and agricultural enterprises. This wide availability not only corrodes nonproliferation but also makes it typically infeasible to identify proliferators by tracking equipment. Facilities that operate this equipment can be as small as a garage or storage room and do not have exceptional power, water, or air conditioning requirements. They do not emit readily detectable pollution or effluents. Testing with laboratory animals or by other means is also normally inconspicuous.

As a result, while a nuclear program is likely to be marked by special mechanisms for handling materials, uniquely configured, large buildings, and readily detectable tests, a biological program is readily concealed. Our record of detection is miserable. A Soviet biological program that employed thousands of people escaped notice until a defector revealed it after almost two decades of operation. A cult attack with salmonella that sickened 600 people in Oregon was ascribed to natural causes until, more than a year later, a defector reported otherwise. Aum Shinrikyo experimented with anthrax and botulinum for 3 years without any awareness by authorities in Japan or elsewhere. Iraq's biological program was little understood before one of Saddam's sons-in-law (and former head of the program) defected, and was grossly overestimated in the years after that source was lost.[18] The 2001 anthrax letter attacks came without warning, and it took a half dozen years and much misdirected effort before the Federal Bureau of Investigation (FBI) identified the source. The dispersion of biological skills and equipment will only intensify difficulties of

---

[17] "[I]t is futile to imagine that access to dangerous pathogens and destructive biotechnologies can be physically restricted, as is the case for nuclear weapons and fissionable materials." National Academy of Sciences, *Biotechnology Research in an Age of Terrorism* (Washington, DC: National Academy of Sciences Press, 2004), 23 (commonly known as the Fink Report).

[18] Bob Drogin, *Curveball: Spies, Lies and the Con Man Who Caused a War* (New York: Random House, 2007), provides a richly detailed account of the most recent chapter in our failures to comprehend Iraq's program—in this case by relying on the accounts of an Iraqi defector who fabricated sensational accounts of a non-existent Iraqi biological weapons program.

detection. A "senior intelligence officer" was right when he told the Commission on Weapons of Mass Destruction that "we do not understand biological weapons better now than five years ago; five years from now, we will understand them less well."[19]

5. Biological material can be transported and disseminated without our knowledge— therefore capturing an attacker is extremely difficult, and he has a powerfully destabilizing capability to "reload" and attack repeatedly.

Weaponized pathogens do not emit signals comparable to those of nuclear materials, which we can detect with Geiger counters and other devices. Because small amounts (a few kilograms or even hundreds of grams) of biological material provide the basis for a catastrophic attack, supplies, whether stored or deployed, are easily hidden. The act of attack is also essentially invisible, whether by an aerosol, or by contaminating food or drink, or by introducing a contagious person or animal into a healthy population. After an attack, the most common method of detection currently used depends on air samples that are routinely sent for laboratory analysis. Typically, these samples will alert us only some 8 to 12 hours after an attack. In addition to suffering from delay, this sampling method does not reveal the location at which an attack was initiated; rather, it registers that air currents have carried a contaminated air sample into the sensor. As a result, an attacker who takes air care to avoid video cameras can remain essentially invisible and be long gone before authorities are even aware that an attack has occurred.

The near invisibility of an attacker combines with the ability to produce significant stockpiles of pathogens (see 2 above) to enable "reload." Our system of homeland defense has focused on incidents—attacks like those on 9/11 that may be surprising and traumatic, but end within hours and permit largely unimpeded recovery. Even the explosion of a nuclear weapon, though devastating, would be an incident. Unless a terrorist stole or produced multiple weapons (an unlikely eventuality), once the attack occurred it would be over, and we would move to issues of restoration and retaliation. But a biological attacker can mount a *campaign*, repeatedly attacking the same target or moving from place to place.[20]

An attack infecting tens of thousands of people one day in New York City, and soon thereafter in Washington, DC, then in San Francisco, St. Louis, and New York again would raise existential problems for this country. We have inadequate capabilities to thwart or to protect ourselves against repeated biological aerosol attacks. Our recovery capabilities are not constructed on this scale. Furthermore, local recovery plans depend on resupply from other parts of the country. A campaign would likely eviscerate these plans as other areas were attacked or anticipated attack and, therefore, more likely demanding rather than supplying assistance.

---

[19] *The Commission on the Intelligence Capabilities of the United States Regarding Weapons of Mass Destruction, Report to the President of the United States* (Washington, DC: Government Printing Office, March 31, 2005), 506, available at <www.gpoaccess.gov/wmd/index.html>.

[20] The 2001 letter attacks provided a small-scale but vivid example of repeated attacks. Had they continued further, it is likely they would have forced closure of the U.S. postal system. At that point, had he continued, the attacker could readily have switched to other means of dissemination. This attribute of bioterrorist attack is acknowledged in the *National Strategy for Countering Biological Threats* (Washington, DC: The White House, November 2009), 15.

6. Attribution of biological attacks is likely to be extremely uncertain; as a result threats of retaliation are not likely to be effective deterrents.

The threat of retribution is likely to be a less effective deterrent against terrorist groups than against states. The relative anonymity of these groups, their territorial dispersion, their willingness to sacrifice themselves and their assets, and their sometimes limited aspirations for affluence, power, or programmatic success after an attack all render them less responsive to the prospects of punitive responses. The availability of pathogens creates a substantial additional difficulty for those who would practice deterrence: unless the attacker announces himself or proceeds in a clumsy manner, it can be difficult to attribute an attack with certainty. If the pathogen occurs naturally, there may be a first challenge even in ascertaining whether an attack has occurred. When an attack is recognized, the collection and analysis of pathogenic material will be a significant second challenge.[21] However, most fundamentally, when that task is completed, it is unlikely to lead to clear-cut attribution. In our one sustained effort to attribute an anonymous attack—the 2001 anthrax letters—the effort took 7 years, and its resolution depended on the fortuity that in a response to a subpoena, the attacker had submitted anthrax samples that uniquely matched the attack samples. If a future weapons developer does not work in laboratories subject to our (or our allies) subpoena power, the same factors that make it difficult to inhibit proliferation, undercut preventive intelligence, and facilitate reload—the widespread availability of pathogens and equipment, the low visibility of production facilities, and the low visibility of an attack—will conjoin to inhibit attribution. Together, these factors undermine deterrence.

The Probability of Bioterrorism

Understandably and reasonably skeptics ask: Why, given the above, have we not seen major traumatic incidents or campaigns of bioterrorism? They also would like a time-phased and disaggregated assessment of the risk. Their urgent questions include: What is the probability that we will confront a major biological attack today or 5 or 10 years from now? What pathogens and modalities of threat pose the greatest risks? Two further questions that are not ordinarily asked, but should be, are: How rapidly is this form of attack likely to proliferate if it is effectively used? How resilient and agile can we be in countering this risk if we wait to act until it evidences itself more forcefully?

These questions cannot be answered confidently. However, the author's best judgment as to the first is that terrorists are both risk averse and imitative. Given a choice between presently familiar explosive weapons and the prospect of developing biological weapons, terrorists will be disinclined to invest in a biological program that requires more time and more resources, and involves more uncertainty. The greater the pressure on a terrorist group (for example, from risk of discovery, or the shutdown of resources), the higher its discount rate is likely to be. Accordingly, most terrorist groups will not incline toward biological weapons.

---

[21] Difficulties in selecting and purifying material are described below.

Instead, we have seen biological programs only from groups (al Qaeda before 9/11, Aum Shinrikyo from 1990–1993, the Rajneeshi cult in the early 1980s) that have a long time horizon, are well funded, and enjoy low visibility or a high degree of sanctuary.

However, it is not ordained that this situation will endure. The Unabomber, for example, was an assistant professor of mathematics at Berkeley who had earned a PhD from the University of Michigan. When he turned misanthropic, he attacked 16 times over 18 years without being captured. During this time, he steadily improved his chosen mode of attack—pipe bombs.[22] There are other attackers of this type.[23] If the next one is a PhD biologist, we may anticipate that he will attack with pathogens rather than pipe bombs. Indeed, the FBI analysis of the fall 2001 anthrax letter attacks is that they were the work of a lone American attacker.

A group analogous to Aum or al Qaeda may also pursue biological weapons, and for the same reasons: they desire a larger and more innovative method of killing, or one that is more enduring or has more economic efffect, so as to better distinguish themselves and capture the attention of their constituencies and/or targets.[24]

No sound calculation can be made as to whether an individual or a group will effectively produce and employ biological weapons within the next decade, year, or month. Indeed, a reader who was so intrepid as to predict the future might do well to reflect that a weapon might have been released yesterday without our yet realizing it.

But the complete uncertainty as to timing should not be equated with improbability. It may be that there is a knee in the curve of bioterrorism: that when some individual or group masters the techniques and attacks repeatedly and effectively, it will inspire others to move in this direction.[25] Kidnapping diplomats, hijacking airplanes, and attacking tourists all had little precedent, but

---

[22] Ted Kaczynski, the Unabomber, "identified closely with the Professor [the protagonist in Joseph Conrad's short story "The Secret Bomber"], who Conrad tells us, lived alone in a 'cramped hermitage' suited to 'the perfect anarchist' where he devoted himself to making 'the perfect detonator.'" See Alston Chase, *A Mind for Murder: The Education of the Unabomber and the Origins of Modern Terrorism* (New York: Norton, 2003), 63.

[23] As another example, see Jeffrey D. Simon, "The Alphabet Bomber (1974)," in *Toxic Terror: Assessing Terrorist Use of Chemical and Biological Weapons*, ed. Jonathan B. Tucker (Cambridge, MA: The MIT Press, 2000), 71–94. For an illuminating discussion of one type of lone terrorist motivation, see Albert Borowitz, *Terrorism for Self-Glorification: The Herostratus Syndrome* (Kent, OH: Kent State University Press, 2005). Herostratus became history's first recorded terrorist when he destroyed one of the Seven Wonders of the World, the Temple of Artemis at Ephesus, in 356 BC, from "a desire for fame or notoriety" (xi).

[24] Violent defenders of animal rights and ecoterrorists, that is, those who practice terrorism to prevent what they take to be destruction of our environment, may be particularly attracted to biological weapons that attack humans but leave the environment and animals intact. For an illuminating example of violence in the name of the environment (but in this case taken against the environment), see John Vaillant, *The Golden Spruce: A True Story of Myth, Madness, and Greed* (New York: Norton, 2006). For a sketch of an effort to argue with (or at least to limit) this moral calculus, see William T. Vollman, *Rising Up and Rising Down: Some Thoughts on Violence, Freedom and Urgent Means* (New York: Ecco, 2003), 506–577.

[25] See generally James Surowiecki, *The Wisdom of Crowds: Why the Many are Smarter than the Few and How Collective Wisdom Shapes Business, Economies, Societies, and Nations* (New York: Random House, 2004), especially 55, 57, 59: "Do cascades exist? Without a doubt. … . There are plenty of occasions when people do closely observe the action of others before making their own decisions. In those cases, cascades are possible, even likely. … Effectively speaking, a few influential people—either because they happened to go first, or because they have particular skills and fill particular holes in people's social networks—determine the course of the cascade." (Footnote reproduced from Danzig, 2008.)

when they dramatically succeeded, they spawned imitations, as though terrorism were a matter of fashion.[26] The transition to a taste for bioterrorism will not be so easy because of the technical requirements,[27] but its coming seems more likely than not.

[26] In *Preparing for Catastrophic Bioterrorism*, 9, I presented data in graphic material to show how sharp rises occurred in kidnappings of tourists and suicide attacks when these became fashionable techniques. For the observation of similar trends in aircraft hijacking, see Robert T. Holden, "The Contagiousness of Aircraft Hijacking," *American Journal of Sociology* 91, no. 4 (1986), 874–904.

[27] For a valuable overview of terrorist groups' assimilation of technological changes, see Brian A. Jackson, *Aptitude for Destruction*, vol. 1, *Organizational Learning in Terrorist Groups and Its Implications for Combating Terrorism* (Santa Monica, CA: RAND, 2005), and Brian A. Jackson et al., *Aptitude for Destruction*, vol. 2, *Case Studies of Organizational Learning in Five Terrorist Groups* (Santa Monica, CA: RAND, 2005).

II. Four Barriers to Progress

Our efforts to come to grips with the risk of bioterrorism are regularly thwarted by organizational fragmentation, distraction, complacency, and the absence of a comprehensive solution. This section analyzes these four barriers. It suggests that they are so deeply embedded in our current circumstances that efforts to directly attack them will fail—indeed, direct attacks are likely to intensify our fragmentation and distraction. Instead, I argue, our best prospect is, counterintuitively, to accept that these difficulties will endure, and to moderate them by constructing a clear, compelling, and limited agenda focused on some essential and unifying points. (section III presents a first attempt at the recommended agenda.)

Fragmentation

There is no doubt that organizational problems impede our coming to grips with the risk of bioterrorism. It has been aptly observed that "homeland security is, at its core, a problem of coordination."[28] Neither the President nor White House staff have the time and depth of immediately available resources to integrate and prioritize actions respecting bioterrorism. A web of laws and directives makes the Secretary of the Department of Homeland Security (DHS) the national "coordinator" of responses to this risk. However, Cabinet secretaries and their subordinates respond to "coordination" by a peer Cabinet secretary and his subordinates only slowly and with great resistance, if at all. The Departments of Health and Human Services (HHS), Justice (including the FBI), Defense, and Agriculture, our 16 intelligence agencies, the Environmental Protection Agency, National Security Council, and Homeland Security Council resist intrusions on their own professional perspectives, concerns, constituencies, congressional relationships, cultures, and priorities.

At different times, the heads of these entities give the problem of bioterrorism different priority. Moreover, to address bioterrorism within their own departments and agencies, these leaders need to marshal quite diverse organizations. The management of DHS, for example, is widely recognized as having difficulty leading its own component parts. Less noted, but no less significantly, HHS, analogously founded in 1980 to coordinate disparate health agencies, has great difficulty coordinating the National Institutes of Health, Biological Advanced Research and Development Agency, Centers for Disease Control and Prevention (CDC), Food and Drug Administration (FDA), Public Health Service, HHS Office of the Assistant Secretary for Emergency Preparedness and Response, and other "subordinate" entities—and this is merely the beginning of a list of those that need to be orchestrated.

---

[28] Donald F. Kettl, *System Under Stress: Homeland Security and American Politics*, 2ᵈ ed. (Washington, DC: CQ Press, 2007), 32.

Cyberterrorism as an Analogous Problem

Though the difficulties described above especially impede effective work on bioterrorism, they are not unique to it. Cyberterrorism—attacking computer software and hardware to disrupt information systems, hence, society—shares with bioterrorism the characteristics of being a relatively new threat born of modern technology and with potentially catastrophic consequences. Like bioterrorism, it can be propagated by states and groups, but also by a lone attacker. As with bioterrorism, the potential for cyberterrorism is spawned by a proliferating technology that does extraordinary good and has become essential, but is subject to misuse in a manner that can be severely damaging.

Though proponents of efforts to address the risks of cyberterrorism might not state their difficulties in this way, they are encountering the four barriers of fragmentation, distraction, complacency, and absence of a comprehensive solution. The fragmentation of responsibility across Federal agencies, between Federal, state, and local governments, and particularly between the private and public sectors has impeded recognition of the cyberterrorism problem just as it has of the problem of bioterrorism. Proponents of initiatives to counter cyberterrorism suffer from undervaluing this risk amid the noise of other threats, from the unfamiliarity and diversity of plausible modes of attack, from the preference of private and public sector constituencies to focus on other pressing concerns (for example, computer reliability rather than security), and from the mistaken expectation that even if a catastrophic cyber attack occurs, we will recover rather readily. As with bioterrorism, efforts to counter cyberterrorism are impeded by professional cultures (for example, the culture of the Internet) that resist government intrusion. And, as with bioterrorism, enthusiasm for work on cyberterrorism is diminished by the lack of comprehensive or singularly effective solutions.

A decade ago I suggested that these new threats might be attended to under an acronym, NEW, standing for nonexplosive warfare. America needs new agendas if it is to adequately recognize and respond to these NEW threats.

The primary responsibility for consequence management lies with governments at the city, regional, and state levels. Moreover, many of the entities—hospitals, clinics, and pharmaceutical companies, for example—that are central to our response lie outside government: they are nonprofit agencies or private corporations. A well-informed observer has lamented that "[t]he nation's health security cannot be built on a foundation of fragmented public health capabilities and capacities any more than our military could be effectively organized as thousands of independent militias."[29]

---

[29] Elin Gursky, "Epidemic Proportions: Building National Public Health Capabilities to Meet National Security Threats: Report to the Subcommittee on Bioterrorism and Public Health Preparedness, Senate Committee on Health, Education, Labor and Pensions" (2005), 2, available at <www.homelandsecurity. org/journal/Epidemic_Proportions_2.pdf>. Gursky also observes: "Public health is organized to serve the health of individual communities with populations in the thousands, not the coordinated health security of a nation of 280 million. The country's public health departments are products of federalism."

Our system of government provides only minimal capacity for coordinating this patchwork of institutions. The difficulties of orchestrating behavior within a Federal agency are raised an order of magnitude by the challenges of working across a score of Federal agencies, raised again by the difficulties of influencing state and local priorities and plans, and made harder still by the need to influence or control private actions. Familiar problems have slowly elicited patterns of coordinated response among these entities.[30] The unfamiliar problem of catastrophic bioterrorism has not catalyzed any such coordination.

The costs of our fragmentation are intensified because nearly all initiatives to counter bioterrorism are of little utility—and indeed can be counterproductive—if they are not integrated with other, quite different, achievements that in turn depend on other professional skills, bureaucracies, and levels of government. For example, in the wake of an aerosol biological attack, sensor systems that sound an alarm will be of low reward (and in fact may encourage panic) if drugs are not stockpiled to cope with the detected pathogen. Even if we have a stockpile of drugs, its value is heavily dependent on our ability to distribute the drugs within a very short time (typically within 48 hours of an attack).[31] Sensors depend on scientists working for DHS; drugs become available only as a result of development, testing, and manufacturing programs conducted by private companies under the oversight of the FDA (a part of HHS); and distribution systems are designed, developed, and operated predominantly by cities and states.

Unfortunately, therefore, single steps by separate actors are both necessary and yet unproductive, and indeed possibly counterproductive if unaccompanied by parallel actions by other actors.

An understandable reaction to this bureaucratic disorder is to call for the creation of a "czar" with directive power capable of addressing the whole problem. Perhaps such a system will arise after a catastrophic bioterrorist attack. But until bioterrorism is manifested as a present, terrifying, existential problem for our republic, efforts at fundamental reorganization are most likely to fail because they run counter to too much inertia, too many deeply embedded interests, and too many cherished ideologies.

For example, our present system is built on the premise of federalism. One manifestation of this is that localities control the response to "catastrophes" like hurricanes, floods, or riots in American cities. Mayors or governors are "in the lead" and the Federal Government provides

---

[30] "Notably absent from the White House process to develop the [Pandemic] Implementation Plan were a number of key stakeholders, including representatives from the States, Territories, Tribes, and localities, as well as the private sector and the international community. . . . As a result, the Executive Branch did not have their buy-in or support. . . . There is limited discussion of the needs of and guidance to the non-Federal public and private sectors in the National Strategy [for Combating Pandemic Influenza] and its Implementation Plan. Other high-level homeland security documents, such as Homeland Security Presidential Directive 10 (Biodefense for the 21st Century . . .) and Homeland Security Presidential Directive 21 (Public Health and Medical Preparedness . . . which identifies problems to be addressed but does not provide direction on how they should be addressed by the non-Federal government) are also oriented towards the Federal government." See House of Representatives Committee on Homeland Security, "Getting Beyond Getting Ready for Pandemic Influenza," Report Prepared by the Majority Staff, January 2009, 7.

[31] Note that this is not synonymous with the time a warning is confirmed from a sensor. Analysis of sensor samples and an actionable judgment that an attack has occurred may consume 24 of the critical 48 hours.

"support." This premise is reflected in our Constitution, in legislation, in Federal agency regulations, supporting plans,[32] and exercises. Unfortunately, as Hurricane Katrina demonstrated, localities often cannot effectively lead the response to wide-area catastrophic events. Responding to a major bioterrorist attack—and particularly to a bioterrorist campaign—is likely beyond the means of any local jurisdiction and will be very different from previously experienced, local events. An anthrax aerosol, for example, can be carried 120 miles by winds and affect many jurisdictions.[33] If reload occurs (or even is feared), a large number of jurisdictions will be making judgments about prophylaxis, decontamination, evacuation, sharing (or not sharing) resources, and other issues. Different judgments (for example, to evacuate from Manhattan, but not to accept potentially contaminated or infected evacuees in Newark, Stamford, or Rye) will be intolerable. Even different advice (for example, to remain at home and vacuum premises in one jurisdiction, but to leave home or, if remaining, not to vacuum in another jurisdiction) will create confusion. The scale and magnitude of events will require Federal direction. But the cultural value of local control makes this proposition taboo, at least in advance of an attack.[34] As a result, we are not realistically preparing for the catastrophes that most demand preparation. For the present, at least, we are doomed to organizational frameworks whose fragmentation inevitably diminishes our present preparation and our future performance.

Distraction

If bioterrorism were the only risk that we faced, it would be easier to organize to cope with it. But this problem is perceived as one among many pressing priorities, and it is highly unlikely that any amount of advocacy will ever give it primacy before a catastrophic attack occurs. Narrowing the window for comparison to terrorist threats does not eliminate the problem. Competing priorities include theft and use of nuclear weapons;[35] attacks on chemical plants and shipments; destruction of power grids; breaches in dams, levees, and reservoirs; cyber attacks on our banks, stock exchanges, governments, and other computer dependent organizations; shoulder-

---

[32] U.S. Department of Homeland Security (DHS), "National Response Framework," January 22, 2008, available at <www.fema.gov/pdf/emergency/nrf/nrf-core.pdf>. And see footnote 36, below.

[33] "Both law enforcement and environmental protection became federal responsibilities [that is, some Federal power was focused in the Federal Bureau of Investigation and Environmental Protection Agency] once policy makers recognized that criminal activity and air and water pollution cross state boundaries. Microbes, of course, don't recognize borders either." Laura H. Kahn, "Unifying the U.S. government response to bioterrorism," *Bulletin of the Atomic Scientists*, December 8, 2008, available at <www.thebulletin.org/web-edition/columnists/laura-h-kahn/unifying-the-us-government-response-to-bioterrorism>.

[34] Documents that might appear as plans are often simply allocations of responsibilities. See, for example, DHS, *The Biological Incident Annex to the National Response Framework* (Washington, DC: DHS, updated August 2008), available at <www.fema.gov/pdf/emergency/nrf/nrf_BiologicalIncidentAnnex.pdf>.

[35] See, for example, Graham Allison, *Nuclear Terrorism: The Ultimate Preventable Catastrophe* (New York: Times Books, 2004), 67–86; Matthew Bunn and Anthony Wier, *Securing the Bomb 2005: The New Global Imperatives* (Cambridge, MA: Nuclear Threat Initiative, May 2005), 27–40.

mounted missiles fired at commercial aircraft—the list may be endless. The possible threats certainly exceed the funds, manpower, and planning capabilities available to counter them.

Even among the constituencies that might particularly focus on biology, bioterrorism is a second-order concern. For decisionmakers besieged by urgent, present health problems, concepts of possible threats in the indefinite future are heavily discounted and rarely receive the time to be understood, much less the resources to address them. Public health professionals, infectious disease doctors, hospital administrators, and leaders of biotechnology and pharmaceutical companies all must meet day-to-day demands from policymakers, members of the public, and their employees and shareholders who are concerned about immediate health challenges already salient in American society (flu, AIDS, drug-resistant tuberculosis, and so forth). Looking beyond the day-to-day, many are understandably less concerned with bioterrorism than they are with the increasing dangers of newly emerging, natural, infectious diseases. Since World War II, novel illnesses have appeared at a rate of almost one every other month.[36] SARS, avian flu, and pandemic influenza[37] are prime examples of this alarming phenomenon. Insofar as bioterrorism claims resources (on the order of $50 billion since 2001),[38] health professionals often see it as a distraction or a source of funding that should be diverted, explicitly or subtly, to more immediate concerns.

Because of their increasing frequency and magnitude, natural disasters also compete for attention among those concerned with emergency planning. It has been calculated that in "the

---

[36] "In the global human population, we report the emergence of 335 infectious diseases between 1940 and 2004. . . . Our database includes [emerging infectious disease] events caused by newly-evolved strains of pathogens (for example, multi-drug-resistant tuberculosis and chloroquine-resistant malaria), pathogens that have recently entered human populations for the first time (for example, HIV-1, severe acute respiratory syndrome (SARS) coronavirus), and pathogens that have probably been present in humans historically, but which have recently increased in incidence (for example, Lyme disease). The emergence of these pathogens and their subsequent spread have caused an extremely significant impact on global health and economies." Kate E. Jones et al., " Global Trends in Emerging Infectious Diseases," *Nature*, vol. 451 (February 21, 2008), 990. For a less quantitative but more descriptive overview, see Laurie Garrett, *The Coming Plague: Newly Emerging Diseases in a World Out of Balance* (New York: Penguin, 1994).

[37] When the United Kingdom established a "National Risk Register" using classified and open source material to assess risks by probability and consequence, it rated a flu pandemic as the number one risk. See John F. Burns, "British Risk Report Says Flu Pandemic Would Have the Most Impact," *The New York Times*, August 9, 2008, available at <www.nytimes.com/2008/08/09/world/europe/09britain.ht ml?tntemail1=y&emc=tnt&pagewanted=print>. Jeffery K. Taubenberger and David M. Morens have calculated that the world fatality rate from the 1918 flu pandemic was 2.5 percent. See "1918 Influenza: The Mother of All Pandemics," *Emerging Infectious Diseases* (January 2006), available at <www.cdc.gov/ ncidod/EID/vol12no01/05-0979.htm>. In 2005 and 2006, the threat of pandemic influenza attracted most of the energy of the U.S. Homeland Security Council, resulting in its promulgation of the "National Strategy for Pandemic Influenza" (November 2005), available at <www.whitehouse.gov/homeland/ pandemic-influenza.html>, and six months later of an "Implementation Plan for the National Strategy for Pandemic Influenza" (May 2006), available at <www.whitehouse.gov/homeland/pandemic-influenza-implementation.html>. The latter document stated that historical data would project 200,000 to 2,000,000 American deaths from such an epidemic (1). Originally the focus in these documents was on H5N1 influenza. More recently, the focus has shifted to H1N1.

[38] Crystal Franco, "Billions for Biodefense: Federal Agency Biodefense Funding, FY2008–FY2009," *Biosecurity and Bioterrorism: Biodefense Strategy, Practice, and Science* 6, no. 2 (June 2008), 131–146.

United States, between 1950 and 1959, there were twenty major disasters costing $38 billion in 1998 dollars. But between 1990 and 1999, there were 82 major disasters, costing $535 billion. . . . [T]he number of disasters multiplied by four, the costs multiplied by fourteen."[39]

Our national security establishment is similarly distracted. While the kinetics of 20th-century warfare led military leaders to make physics, chemistry, mathematics, and engineering staples of their professional educations, biology—even as it was understood in the 20th century—was not a part of the education of most of our senior decisionmakers. An astute historian noted that World War I can be described as the era of assimilation of chemistry into warfare; World War II saw the integration of physicists; the Cold War brought computer science and telecommunications to the fore.[40] There has not yet been an era of integration for biology.[41]

Military unfamiliarity is compounded by our appropriate renunciation of biological offensive programs 40 years ago. As a result, many of our concepts about how these weapons might be used are outdated and limited. Within the Armed Forces, biology has been left to the medical commands; it is regarded as "a support activity," not a branch of warfare. Even specialized military and police units devoted to WMD or NBC defense have historically been trained predominantly in nuclear and chemical matters, not biological. In *NBC*, the *B* is silent.

These problems can be mitigated by educating professionals, government leaders, and members of the public about biological terrorism. We have made some progress, particularly after President Bill Clinton took a personal interest in the issue in 1998, as did Vice President Richard Cheney after the attacks in 2001. At a lesser level, this paper and other writings are obviously efforts to garner more attention to this issue. But we must recognize that, even with leadership interest at the highest levels and vigorous educative efforts, bioterrorism has remained and will remain a marginal issue on the national agenda until a catastrophic attack occurs.

Complacency

America suffers from a Pearl Harbor syndrome, not simply, or even predominantly, in the sense that it fears surprise. When confronted by a welter of threats, we unconsciously discount the costs of being unprepared because we believe that, even if we are unprepared, the resilience of America will assert itself, as it did after Pearl Harbor. The result is a dangerous tolerance of inadequate preparedness. Without ever saying it, we assume that we may well be surprised, but, as with Pearl Harbor and 9/11, a resilient America will absorb the shock and respond in a muscular

---

[39] Charles Perrow, *The Next Catastrophe: Reducing Our Vulnerabilities to Natural, Industrial, and Terrorist Disasters* (Princeton: Princeton University Press, 2007), 15. Unfortunately, Perrow, an emeritus professor of sociology at Yale University, does not provide footnotes documenting this calculation.

[40] Alan D. Beyerchen, "From Radio to Radar: Interwar Military Adaptation to Technological Change in Germany, the United Kingdom, and the United States," in *Military Innovation in the Interwar Period*, ed. Williamson R. Murray and Allan R. Millett (Cambridge: Cambridge University Press, 1996), 265–299.

[41] This also affects those outside government. Academics and private sector employees with professional training in physics and chemistry broadly accept principles of security classification and the imperatives of preparation for disaster, such as nuclear and chemical plant accidents. No such tradition exists within biology. There is more resistance to Federal intrusion into this field, whether through restrictions on publication and research activities or through cooperation on intelligence matters.

and effective manner; that, however traumatic, the incident of the moment will be no more than an incident. But biological attackers' capacities for reload, and the likelihood that fashion will trigger second entrants (and third and fourth and fifth entrants), risk combining with the long lead time for construction of defenses to make us unusually vulnerable to bioterrorism. There may be no period for recovery. Rather, we may be subject to a campaign, even an expanding campaign, for which, if we have not prepared, we will have no response.

The Pearl Harbor syndrome is probably too deeply embedded in our experience and our psyches to be directly countered. At a minimum, however, those who are not complacent about the risks of bioterrorism should prepare for the moment when a catastrophic attack will shatter that complacency. For example, it may be impossible and a diversion of resources to attempt to get citizens to focus on preparation for a bioterrorist attack before a major one occurs. But it is irresponsible not to prepare the messages that would be conveyed to citizens after the attack, when their attention will be intensely focused.

Absence of a Comprehensive Solution

Two of the most common metaphors in Washington parlance state that policymakers gravitate to low-hanging fruit, and that they look for their keys under light posts. In our efforts to counter bioterrorism, we have found that no fruit hangs low, and solutions lie in darkness. Almost every initiative—smallpox vaccination, anthrax vaccination, controls on publication, creation of environmental sampling and alarm systems, expansion of intelligence work, consequence management planning, drug research, development and acquisition—has been imperfectly understood, contentious, difficult to execute, and at best imperfectly successful. This is in part a consequence of the fragmentation of the problem, but it also results from the novelty of the problem.

Policymakers often resist action because they crave a comprehensive solution, be it an intelligence capability, a control mechanism, an omnivalent vaccination, or some other magical mechanism for resolving the problem. We need to accept that no one now knows how to comprehensively cope with bioterrorism. Moreover, we need to recognize that this is not just the result of the novelty of the issues. It is likely to be an enduring characteristic of the risk.

In the past, we have been stymied by the remarkable availability and variety of biological material and the means of distributing it in infectious form.[42] This continues to be the case. But at the dawn of the 21st century, the problem is compounded, and in the years ahead it will grow worse because biotechnology permits the creation of new or modified organisms. This will generate new threats that attackers can use to circumvent any single defense.

Cutting-edge biologists see this vividly, but our bureaucracies only dimly. Bioterrorism is a 21st-century threat that must be acted on by decisionmakers whose mindsets have been shaped by 20th-century experience. Even enlightened leaders must cope with the fact that bureaucracies focus on repetitive tasks designed to cope with the world as it was when they were created. Organizations adapt too slowly to afford ready protection against a rapidly changing world.

---

[42] For example, the technique employed in the French and Indian War of embedding smallpox virus in blankets could now be applied by giving similarly infected blankets to the homeless, or by infecting suicide terrorists, or, more effectively, by using an aerosol sprayer. The virus that causes foot and mouth disease in cattle and pigs poses a very different threat from the bacterium that causes anthrax in humans, and the anthrax bacterium itself comes in a hundred different strains, some benign and others quite virulent. Some pathogens are contagious, but others are not. Most deteriorate rapidly in the air, but some do not. Some weapons would most effectively be delivered as outdoor aerosols, but other means of delivery (as in the food supply or indoors) can be effective, and for some weapons at some times, the alternatives are more effective. Though we are able to detect many pathogens relatively quickly, others could elude detection for a substantial time. For some pathogens we have effective drugs; for a smaller number effective vaccines; but many pathogens are subject to modifications that can circumvent drugs (it is harder to circumvent vaccines), and for some pathogens, we have no effective drugs or vaccines. As a result, it is hard to formulate comprehensive strategies.

III. Top 10 Recommendations for Action

Top 10 lists may be taken too lightly because they carry the connotations of transitory bestseller lists or late night television jokes. If taken seriously, their construction may also be a distraction, degenerating into arguments about whether they omit too much or include too much, or how a particular point should be phrased. A short list can, however, be a catalyst for change. A defined, clear, and limited set of recommendations can help counter the difficulties described in the preceding section. Such a list can be a basis for common agreement that counters *fragmentation*. If the entries on the list are understood as imperatives, they can offset *complacency* and *distraction*. And, though the list does not provide a *comprehensive resolution* to the risks of bioterrorism, it can provide a map to progress in many directions, offsetting the sense that there is no path to credible progress.

This list is not designed to denigrate ongoing efforts. Rather, it is intended to highlight the things that in my judgment are vital but neglected. They are the top 10 things that must happen if we are to prepare for bioterrorism, but in the main are not happening and will not happen, absent leadership.

These recommendations are intended as a starting point. Optimally, they will first be used to catalyze discussion in which other experts will express their views and suggest reformulations, removals, and replacements among our top 10 priorities. (It will, however, be desirable to preserve the discipline of limiting the list to 10.) This process should then yield consensus or an understanding of disagreements about proposed new priorities. With this understanding, these recommendations should become a subject for decision by relevant government policymakers. Each of the agenda items self-consciously should be either rejected or embraced. Budgets, policies, regulations, exercises, and the other stuff of bureaucracy should follow accordingly. After some time, the resulting list should provide a baseline for assessing progress and considering revision in our priorities. Within 1 or 2 years, a further review might appropriately conclude that some of the initiatives that were embraced will have been accomplished, others demand continued leadership attention, and a third category may be judged to be irrelevant or futile.

These entries are not presented in priority order. Instead, they start with the most particular points and continue on to higher levels of generality. This order also corresponds with a movement from shorter term initiatives to those that require more time. In my judgment, however, all demand urgent attention starting now.

1. Develop an immediately usable, detailed plan for coping with catastrophic attacks in one city that is especially at risk.

Since 9/11, several efforts to create a Federal framework for state and local emergency response have yielded limited benefits. These efforts have focused on allocating responsibilities among government organizations.[43] Secondarily, they have in some instances involved Federal agency "assessment" of "gaps" in state and local programs.[44] This division of roles and missions and assessment of progress is useful, but does not develop actual plans as to how we would respond to particular challenges in unprecedented emergencies.

Documentary annexes and 1- or 2-day exercises built around bioterrorist scenarios provide some depth, but are not a substitute for comprehensive detailed planning. Furthermore, a "one size fits all" approach that plans at a national level fails to energize local jurisdictions to examine their particular requirements and locks our plans at a lowest common denominator that localities are willing to embrace. The result is that our present plans do not grapple with such basic issues as whether, after detecting anthrax in an air sample, we would evacuate or have people stay in place, whether we would deploy response personnel without protective equipment, how we would resupply contaminated areas, and so forth. These deficiencies are indefensible and will powerfully amplify the effects of an attack.

It will be objected that particular decisions will need to be made in the light of particular information. But it is highly likely that in a real incident very little particular information will be available when these decisions will have to be made. (For example, we are likely to have no more than an alarming indication that anthrax has been discovered in our sampling devices.) More detailed plans should at least presumptively address key issues now because we have time to consider their many aspects; our prior consideration would enable us to move more quickly in an emergency; we could develop resources and plans to help us carry out our likely decisions; and identifying likely actions will help determine priorities for our longer term research, development, and acquisition programs.

A useful innovation would supplement the general plan with a detailed collaboration with a single jurisdiction that is particularly at risk and, as a result of that risk, is particularly committed to planning and preparing in detail.[45] Plans with that jurisdiction (optimally, New York City) should posit one or two particular risks from bioterrorism, which can be drawn from present national planning scenarios. Federal and local planners should then, in considerable detail, walk through the decisions that will need to be made in response to an attack (evacuation, operation of mass transit, means of decontamination, support of nonresident transients, and so forth). Federal-state-

---

[43] The National Response Framework (a new name for what was previously called the National Response Plan) lays out the basics. The framework and related documents can be found at the Federal Emergency Management Agency's (FEMA) National Response Framework (NRF) Resource Center, available at <www.fema.gov/emergency/nrf/>.

[44] For the most developed assessment, see Department of Health and Human Services (HHS) and DHS, "Assessment of States' Operating Plans to Combat Pandemic Influenza," December 2008, available at <www.pandemicflu.gov/plan/states/state_assessment.html>.

[45] Initial planning of this kind should be with a jurisdiction that volunteers to participate. If the experiment is successful, future efforts can condition the flow of Federal assistance relevant to bioterrorism to the promulgation of these plans. The principal mechanism for this assistance is through the Centers for Disease Control's Public Health Emergency Preparedness Agreements, which provided over $700 million in 2008 to 62 state and local public health departments. These agreements include performance metrics, but they focus on distribution of drugs and mobilization of health professionals and not on the range of activities described in this paper.

city agreement on these steps (agreement that is lacking now) can then be used as a basis for similar discussion and planning with neighboring jurisdictions (for example, Connecticut and New Jersey), for analogous discussions with other jurisdictions at high risk (Washington, DC), and for enriching the general plan (which now exists at too high a level of abstraction).

2. Establish realistic and effective Federal-local interactions.

In some respects Federal and local responsibilities for coping with bioterrorism are well defined, in others ill defined; in some respects relative responsibilities are hotly debated; other issues, indeed fundamental issues, are little discussed.

Among the well-defined matters, scientific and drug-related issues benefit from an understanding of the division of responsibilities between different government agencies. Drug development, screening, regulation, acquisition, and stockpiling are Federal responsibilities. In the wake of a bioterrorist attack, the Federal Government would be responsible for bulk distribution from its stockpiles to the affected area. From there, states and localities are responsible for distribution to affected residents within 48 hours. No city meets this standard, but the allocation of responsibility is clear.

As another example of reasonable clarity about responsibilities, if a Biowatch sample captures a pathogen suggesting a terrorist attack, a federally coordinated system of local laboratories analyzes samples, and the CDC and the Biological Analysis Center will be looked to (as they were at the time of the 2001 anthrax letters) for authoritative characterization of samples.

Relationships on less technical matters are, however, much less clear, particularly as they concern attack characterization, public communication, and high-consequence decisions about attack response. The Biowatch detection system, since its inception in 2002, has been a Federal responsibility, and Federal regulators have attempted even to prevent localities from developing independent systems of aerosol sampling. However, authorities in New York City have recently asserted that they have the right to control the systems within their jurisdiction, for example by relocating scarce detection resources to suit their own population protection priorities. Less discussed has been a yet more important function: how do local and Federal authorities interact when laboratory assessments indicate that a sample shows the presence of a pathogen that is normally associated with biological attack?[46]

The federally promulgated National Response Framework allocates to the local mayor the responsibility for declaring an attack in this situation.[47] It is hard to believe, however, that many mayors would be either much inclined or well positioned to make this judgment. On the other hand, few if any mayors would tolerate a judgment that was made without their participation, particularly as this judgment would have immense effects. On the one hand, a false alarm would be hugely disruptive; on the other hand, a failure to alarm could result in thousands, tens of thousands, or even hundreds of thousands of potentially avoidable deaths.

In such highly freighted situations, most political actors and bureaucratic systems default to discussion—they attempt to find consensus so that information is pooled, diverse consequences

---

[46] For example, smallpox, which no longer exists in nature, or anthrax, which can be pervasive in cattle raising areas but would not normally be present in aerosolized forms in urban areas.

[47] See the FEMA NRF Resource Center at <www.fema.gov/emergency/nrf/>.

are considered, and (*above all*) no party bears sole responsibility for so momentous a decision. A collaborative decision would indeed be desirable after an indication of a biological attack, if time permitted. However, if an attack has occurred, every minute of discussion will delay the distribution of drugs and, therefore, increase the number of deaths. Delay will also add to the numbers of those who enter contaminated areas, those who leave and may carry contamination, and those who travel to areas where they may be less likely to receive treatment. Furthermore, so many people would have at least partial information pointing to an attack that leaks, public rumors amplified by Internet communication, and public pressures would mount exponentially with passing minutes. This situation will exact a heavy price for confusion and delay in executing responsibilities.

Subsequent decisions will have the same characteristics: though slightly more time and information may be available, high uncertainty and the pressure for speedy decisions will remain. Fatigue, tension, and the death toll will increase. The conditions of decisionmaking will be like those we associate with war. However, our decisionmaking system has none of the attributes we have learned are necessary in war: hierarchies among would-be decisionmakers; clarity about the powers delegated to each; command, control, and information systems that conform to the distribution of responsibilities; and extensive training so that all participants can perform their roles under pressure. Do these qualities in any way characterize the likely postattack relationships between the mayors of San Francisco, Oakland, and Berkeley, the Governor of California, the Secretary of Homeland Security, the Secretary of Health and Human Services, and the head of the FBI?

After a catastrophic biological attack, the price of fragmentation will be delay. In addition to delay, fragmentation will assuredly cause confusion. If the cities of San Francisco, Berkeley, and Oakland are all affected (or their officials believe they may be affected), each mayor has to make a judgment as to whether and how to permit ingress and egress from his jurisdiction, and underneath each mayor, with limited or no guidance from him, each police force, transit department, emergency services unit, and public health system will have to decide how to allocate resources, advise and direct its employees, advise and support its citizens and transients, and control its citizens and transients within its jurisdiction. To the extent that these decisions are incompatible, confusion and tension will increase. If the mayor of San Francisco encourages or orders evacuation, and the mayor of Oakland seeks to minimize contamination by restricting transients, or the Bay Area Rapid Transit system shuts down its systems, what should be consequence management will become chaos. Similarly, if local health authorities provide contradictory advice (stay indoors/go outdoors; vacuum/do not vacuum), citizens' concerns will be amplified.

Beyond problems of inconsistency of direction and advice lie problems of insufficiency of resources. Many scenarios presume 100,000 infections from a single attack. DHS planning factors presume that 10 times as many "worried well" will seek medical assistance as are actually infected in these situations. Neither premise has a strong basis in data and analysis[48]—but both are plausible and appropriately suggestive of the scale of demands for help. Against the potential demand on the order of one million people, the total flow-through in emergency rooms in the Washington Metropolitan Area (including adjacent Maryland and Northern Virginia) is approximately 3,250

---

[48] I discuss the analytic underpinnings in Richard J. Danzig, "Reload and Its Implications," paper prepared for the DARPA Defense Sciences Office (DSO), September 2004, particularly notes 22–24.

patients per day.[49] Some factors may mitigate the mismatch: hospitals might surge to twice their normal capacities; potential patients would perhaps spread themselves over several days; triage systems might improve the speed with which patients could be seen. But the magnitude of the mismatch should be evident.

Similar problems would arise for police and local National Guard resources. Travel restrictions, a need to attend to their families, illness from exposure, and fear of their own infection might reduce the numbers of those available for duty. Police are often triple-counted: they are not only policemen but also off-duty security guards (including for hospitals) and members of the National Guard. But even if none of these factors apply, even large and very professional local police forces cannot be expected to meet the magnitude of demands to protect important facilities, maintain order, assist citizens, enforce essential laws, participate in efforts to thwart potential attackers, and participate in efforts to investigate the attack or attacks that have already occurred.

Evidently, after a biological attack the Federal role will be much more than merely supportive. It cannot be said, however, that the Federal Government is prepared for this role. The most striking case in point is in the provision of Active duty military to provide security, logistics, and medical support to an affected city. Recently, there has been a commendable acceptance of a homeland security mission for DOD—at least as an option of last resort. A combatant command (U.S. Northern Command [USNORTHCOM]) has been charged with this mission and has established procedures for estimating troop requirements and tasking another command (U.S. Joint Forces Command [USJFCOM]) with supplying the required resources. However, these developments merely provide a bureaucratic path for action. They do not develop the capabilities to effectively take this action. The military, as I have argued elsewhere,[50] is not, and cannot be regarded as, a deus ex machina—a magical solution whose invocation will resolve previously intractable problems. The core of military capability is not predominantly in the manpower or equipment DOD brings to bear, but rather in the strategic and tactical planning it brings to its mission, the training it provides before deployment, and the situational awareness it brings to bear when adapting its training and planning to the particular circumstances in which it operates. When these are lacking (as, for example, in Iraq in 2002–2004), our military, capable though it is, is unlikely to succeed in its missions.

Seen from this perspective, the military preparation for a bioterrorist attack is not encouraging. The supporting command (USJFCOM) has not designated, and has no plans to designate, specific units for the USNORTHCOM homeland security mission. As a result, units will in no respect be specially trained or equipped for these missions. For its part, the supported command (USNORTHCOM) has not demanded military training and equipment for civilian consequence management after a bioterrorist attack because it has not analyzed the likely requirements in anything other than a top-line fashion (that is, X hospital beds, Y doctors). Nor have steps been taken to facilitate the exchange of information with civilian agencies and the development of systems that would provide situational awareness.

---

[49] Richard J. Danzig, Rachel Kleinfeld, and Philipp Bleek, *After an Attack: Preparing Citizens for Bioterrorism* (Washington, DC: Center for New American Security, 2007), appendix 1, 41.

[50] Richard J. Danzig, "Preparing for Bioterrorism: Operating in the Fourth Dimension," paper prepared for the DARPA DSO, October 2007.

This is despite the fact that, when it assessed the performance of all Federal agencies in the wake of Hurricane Katrina, the U.S. House of Representatives singled out the "blinding lack of situational awareness and disjointed decision-making [that] needlessly compounded and prolonged Katrina's horror."[51]

Rich development of a particular city plan, as urged in the previous recommendation, can illuminate these problems and provide a template for other cities. But as that particular plan is developed, a broader review of Federal roles needs to be undertaken, and our expectations and preparations need to become more realistic.

3. Upgrade our abilities to assess aerosol attacks.[52]

Familiar questions of criminal investigation ("who? what? where? and when?") will be raised after a biological attack. But the urgency with which these questions will be asked, the reasons for asking them, and the means of addressing them will be outside our normal experience. Faced with these issues after the most devastating form of biological attack—outdoor aerosol dissemination—it is likely that we will be catastrophically unprepared to investigate them and slow, uncertain, and very probably wrong in the answers that we will provide. It is imperative that we understand this deficiency and its consequences and immediately move to correct it.

We undervalue this problem because the terrorist attacks that have shaped our priorities in recent years have permitted reasonably rapid and reliable situational assessment. After terrorists struck with guns and explosive devices in places as diverse as Oklahoma City, London, Jerusalem, and Mumbai, the authorities, though greatly stressed, were able to achieve an adequate situational understanding within hours. Physical damage was evident, most citizens could quickly ascertain their own injury or well-being, and the location of the attackers was relatively clear. In each case, the incident clearly ended with the death (frequently suicide) or capture of the assailants. The 9/11 attacks generated greater uncertainty, but within hours it was apparent what had happened, and that further attacks by this means could be thwarted by shutting down air flights. Within days, it was evident who was responsible, and that both short- and longer term countermeasures could control the risk of aviation attacks.

Bioterrorism is different. Unless attackers provide us with the gift of announcing and precisely and credibly describing what they have done, a bioterrorist aerosol attack is not likely to be recognized for many hours or some days. When it is recognized, the pathogen could be unclear (Was this anthrax?) and its precise attributes (What strain of anthrax? Has it been engineered, for example, to achieve resistance to some or many antibiotics?) are likely to be unknown. The time of initiation of attack will probably only approximately be estimated, its point of origin obscure, its duration unknown, the quantity of pathogen distributed unascertainable, and the mechanism

---

[51] House Select Bipartisan Committee to Investigate the Preparation for and Response to Hurricane Katrina, "A Failure of Initiative," 109th Cong., 1st Sess. (2005), available at <http://Katrina.house.gov/>.
[52] Food, water, and animal inspection systems provide equivalent safeguards in the event of nonaerosol attacks. Attacks through these media are likely to be delayed (because of distribution systems), more limited, and more readily recognized and assessed than attacks through the less familiar and more immediately disseminated form of aerosol sprays. Accordingly, improvements of mechanisms of detection and assessment in food, water, and animals are not a focus of my first priority recommendations. Others may argue for giving them higher priority.

of distribution uncertain. As a result, we will be ignorant about who can confidently be said to be infected, which facilities, areas, and people are contaminated, whether repeat attacks are occurring, where and by what means attacks could be expected to recur, and how to protect ourselves against that recurrence. Uncertainty will be compounded because biological agents are invisible, can be carried great distances by winds (anthrax could be carried over a hundred miles), and because repeat attacks or line attacks (continuous spraying from cars or airplanes for example) can cause wide and discontinuous contamination. Because the evidence of the attack (samples in our detectors or clinical reports of illness) is dissociated from the time and place of its initiation, we are also not likely to know much, if anything, about the attacker.

To improve our safety, three related, but quite distinct, tasks must be mastered. We need capabilities to detect attacks, to determine the attacker (attribution), and to establish situational awareness sufficient to guide our consequence management activities. Our efforts since 2001 have created stubby, inadequate, and frail versions of the first two legs of this triad, but they have at least begun to be built and yield real benefit. The third leg is close to nonexistent and demands urgent attention.

Detection. There is good reason to have made detection a priority. Pathogens are invisible and ordinarily have delayed effects. Even when they enter our bodies, they typically take 2 or more days to produce symptoms. When symptoms appear, it is often too late effectively to aid those who are infected. For this reason, air sampling detectors (Biowatch), clinical reporting systems (Biosense), a "response network" of 160 laboratories,[53] and intelligence collection systems all have warranted the investments made in recent years. They increase the probability that we will detect an aerosol attack before its symptomatic effects are apparent.

Inadequacies in our efforts are generally recognized. There are too few detectors,[54] too widely spread, with too much delay in manual collection and analysis (typically 12 hours), and there is too much reliance on the assumption that a single positive event (a "Biowatch actionable report") should and will trigger an immediate and severely disruptive response.

These limitations are being considered and significantly addressed by the introduction of automated, near-instantaneous detection systems, by the reconsideration of responses, and by nascent thinking about how to train decisionmakers to assess and respond to actionable reports. All of these topics need attention from policymakers, but, with two exceptions, this attention can be devoted to accelerating the present trajectory rather than altering its course.

The first exception is that new policymakers would be well advised to press for order-of-magnitude cost reductions so as to multiply air sampling devices and consequently promote detection from sparse to widespread coverage. This might be accomplished by moving device development and production from national laboratories to industrial partners more accustomed to price competition, by pressing for economies of scale, or by experimenting with alternative forms of detection (for example, systems built into heating, ventilation, and air conditioning systems). Detection arrays that were both more densely and more widely distributed would increase the risk of individual sampler error (there would be more samplers), but they would permit demanding

---

[53] The CDC estimates that in 2007, 90 percent of Americans lived within 100 miles of a Laboratory Response Network participant. See *Public Health Preparedness: Strengthening CDC's Emergency Response* (Washington, DC: CDC, January 2009), 24, available at <www.bt.cdc.gov/publications/jan09phprep/pdf/jan09phprep.pdf>.

[54] Precise numbers are classified.

multiple hits before initiating major responses, and they would provide much more precision in recognizing the scale and origin of an attack.

Beyond this, more attention needs to be paid to the linkage between confirmed detection and policymakers' responses. The present system is premised on the willingness of mayors, the President, and others to take so-called high regret actions, like shutting down a city on the basis of a judgment by a single laboratory official confirming the likely reliability and accuracy of the detection. Training will be useful. At a minimum, officials in the Obama administration will need to be familiar with and accepting of this premise. We need, however, to move beyond this. Key officials should challenge this premise and, through close inquiry and some exercises, decide whether there are opportunities for rendering the system less dependent on single, hair-trigger judgments.

Attribution. As described above, if we are to deter attacks, we need to have an apparent capability to assess an aerosol and trace it back to its place of origin. If we are to prevent repeat future attacks, we need to know whatever can be known about the means of distribution that was employed and the character of the attacker(s).

In an insightful report published in the summer of 2001,[55] the Defense Science Board placed high priority on the development of forensic tools for assessing biological attacks. The anthrax letter attacks of 2001 gave this immediate operational significance when unusually capable leaders in the FBI recognized that they needed a new science—microbial forensics—to analyze the anthrax spores in envelopes and compare them with known repositories of similar material. By this means, over the course of 7 years, the FBI determined where the *b. anthracis* used in these attacks came from and developed essential clues as to the perpetrator. Specifically, they determined that the *b. anthracis* employed in these attacks was from an Ames strain with four unusual mutations. These mutations were found in one and only one flask in the laboratory of a chief suspect. More traditional investigative tools enhanced the case against this suspect.[56]

While there is some dispute about the outcome, the value of microbial forensics is now well recognized, and an organization—the National Bioforensics Center at the National Biological Assessment and Analysis Center—has been established to develop and practice this science. Moreover, the Intelligence Community has taken the lead in developing an interagency task force to establish research, training, and other investment priorities in this field.

Bioforensic tools are essential because in future attacks we are unlikely to have the benefit of three fortuities that were fundamental to tracking the 2001 attacker. The first is time. It took 7 years and several mistakes to identify the perpetrator; it would be intolerable if attacks were continuing and we could not attribute them to any individual, group, or country over a period of months or years.

Second, in the 2001 attacks we had the benefit of pristine samples preserved in envelopes. An aerosol attack will generate small samples from our air filter systems, pathogens in transmuted forms in the bodies of victims, and larger and more representative, but contaminated, samples

---

[55] "Report of the Defense Science Board/Threat Reduction Advisory Committee Task Force on Biological Defense."

[56] A good account may be found in "Tracing Killer Spores," *Analytical Chemistry*, September 18, 2008. See also <http://anthraxvaccine.blogspot.com/2008/09/additional-comments-by-dr-popov-on.html>. The *Analytical Chemistry* article concludes: "Undoubtedly, the investigation of the anthrax mailings put the field of microbial forensics on the map."

"scraped" from walls, floors, clothing, and equipment in affected areas. It is likely that this material will be more corrupted and confusing than in the 2001 case.

Third, the resolution of the 2001 case depended on not only the analysis of the material used in the attack, but also the comparison of this anthrax with anthrax stocks inventoried in U.S. laboratories and then subpoenaed from them. If in future attacks the source material is hidden (inside the United States or outside it), the case will not admit of resolution by comparison.

For these reasons, we need a robust and innovative microforensics program that goes beyond the FBI's substantial achievement. The outline of the strategy for development of this leg of the triad is reasonably determined. Policymakers' contributions should be addressed primarily to assuring interagency attention and cooperation, and to doubling or tripling the funding from present levels of approximately twenty million dollars per year.

Situational Awareness. Biowatch is not a system that provides attack assessment, that is, illumination about the origins of an attack, its precise timing, and so forth. Modeling efforts can supplement the system, but there are too many unknowns to permit models—developed for use in events known to have occurred in precise times and places, as, for example, Three Mile Island—to be effective. For consequence management to be effective, attack assessment needs to be elevated as a priority, and manpower and funds allocated to technologies and plans that will provide urgently needed information in a timely manner.[57]

Situational awareness is especially required for outdoor aerosol attacks not only because these can most rapidly affect the largest number of people, but also, and even more significantly, because urban microclimates vary so substantially across place and time that the exposures and contaminations can be large and difficult to ascertain. The 2001 anthrax letters also demonstrate that other forms of attack can generate highly disruptive consequences and very difficult challenges for situational awareness. A few contaminated letters, foods, or medicines can induce uncertainty about the entire supply. It is the uncertainty, not the attack, that will severely limit or shut down vital systems, induce fear, and divert resources.

We need to assess an attack's character, magnitude, time of initiation, points of initiation, geographic areas of infection and contamination, and clues as to how to apprehend its perpetrators, or at least thwart further attacks by them. We need to know, for example, not only that anthrax has been released, but also whether it is resistant to antibiotics—and therefore whether first responders should or should not be sent to contaminated places with only antibiotic protection. We need to know whether an aerosol attack at a particular street in Manhattan spreads predominantly or exclusively west, east, north, or south, extends to all of the borough or to much of the rest of New York City, or to an area that sprawls well beyond New York and perhaps encompasses hundreds of square miles in surrounding states. We need to know not just that a pathogen was discovered at 10 a.m., but also whether it was present and may have infected commuters during the earlier morning

---

[57] Opportunities include, for example, lidar systems (such as now used by the Pentagon) to detect aerosol clouds in real time with tightly defined places of origin, decentralized automated detection systems (for example, in building filtration systems), sampling methods and procedures that can reliably and quickly measure ground contamination in affected areas, and rapid diagnostics that can confidently establish who has or has not been infected. Technology development needs to be followed by acquisition and by training programs that will help relevant officials practice making attack assessments under conditions of ambiguity and pressure.

rush hour, or indeed the rush hour the evening before. We need to know what areas are clean and can therefore safely be used for transport, treatment, and staging.

Put generally, our situational awareness must improve. We can move in this direction by increasing the number of detectors, as described above. In addition, expanding the law enforcement/attribution focus in the microbial forensics program will contribute to aspects of situational awareness. In the first critical hours after a biological attack, absent extraordinary luck or a self-defeating choice by the attacker to identify himself, our main (and perhaps only) clue will be the pathogen captured in an air sampling detector. Accordingly, a major research and development effort should be initiated to enhance the speed, reliability, and scope of material collection, handling, and analysis. Prime goals should include shortening the present 1- to 2-day period for assessing antibiotic resistance; developing more rapid, reliable, and rewarding plans for collecting and analyzing samples from collection points other than Biowatch detectors; and conceiving and testing methods for drawing inferences from material, not only about its threat to health, but also about how, by whom, and where it was created and distributed.

In sum, two legs of our triad must be made stronger, the third needs to be created, and all three must be better integrated. Until this is done, we will be inadequately prepared for biological defense.

4. Build interdiction capabilities.

The great weight of our efforts against bioterrorism seeks to cope with two important and evident problems: how to prevent an attack and how to mitigate the consequences if an attack occurs. But there is a third, somewhat more subtle, but actually more important problem that receives almost no attention. This is the challenge of preventing repeat attacks after the first attack has occurred. An individual biological attack can be deadly, traumatic, and destructive, but a campaign of repeated attacks can do things that no individual attack will accomplish. A campaign of bioterrorism can debilitate our ability to function as an economy and as a government.

The problem has been outlined in the discussion of reload in section I. Readily accessible technologies will enable a terrorist to produce pathogens in quantities that will support repeated attacks, to attack invisibly, and to reload, move, wait a while, and attack again. Our highest priority should be to have the capability to prevent campaign terrorism by capturing an attacker, or at least thwarting his mode of attack.

We do not have this capability. More remarkably, we are making almost no effort to develop it. In part, this is because it is a technically hard problem. Indeed, it is a "wicked problem" that will require coordination of several disciplines (physics, biology, law enforcement, meteorology, mathematical modeling, and forensics among them). No less fundamentally, it is a problem that will require bureaucratic focus to overcome problems of fragmentation. DHS defines its bioterrorism missions around detection and consequence management; HHS gives priority to drug development, stockpiling, and distribution; DOD is concerned with battlefield protection and incidental homeland security support. The FBI is admirably developing a forensic program designed to permit conviction of a perpetrator, but it is not oriented toward preventing crimes, and has neither the mandate nor the resources for a research program to deal with the unprecedented problem of interdicting a repeat biological attacker.

Elsewhere I have suggested (or encouraged others to suggest)[58] the start of approaches to this problem. They include new detection technologies,[59] much denser distribution of existing automated detectors with the aim of detecting an attacker (not simply, as now, of detecting an attack),[60] improved abilities to assess the material used in an attack (as described in the previous recommendation),[61] and better planning for restrictions that could be imposed after an attack (limiting aerosol spraying and vehicle movement at times and places of special concern).

Bureaucracies are more or less adept at performing functions for which they have established structures, organized programs, and employed staff. They have great difficulty, however, perceiving how new problems require new programs and investments. Accordingly, the most important function of leaders is to set new agendas for work by subordinate bureaucracies. The problem of thwarting campaign bioterrorism is very possibly existential. It is not being addressed. There is no more important challenge for a leader in this arena than to initiate imaginative and sustained work on this problem.

5. Build decontamination capabilities.

Our plans to manage the consequences of the use of weapons of mass destruction have focused on mitigating amounts and consequences of death and violent destruction. More subtle are the problems of contamination that might follow the use of these weapons.

Such planning as does occur for coping with these difficulties has been developed primarily in the context of nuclear and chemical materials.[62] The risks of contamination are well understood from nuclear power plant analyses, transport accidents in the chemical industry, and weapons effect assessments in the military. Some biological weapons would also pose severe contamination problems.[63] All would deteriorate in sunlight, but because *b. anthracis* is protected as a spore, it poses enduring risks of persistent contamination in covered, even shaded, places. Even much more vulnerable viruses (like the virus that causes smallpox) and bacteria (like the bacterium that causes plague) could be expected to persistently contaminate closed environments like subway, commuter rail, and automobile tunnels. These environments would need to be assessed for contamination

---

[58]   Richard J. Danzig, "Reload and the Post-Attack Environment," unpublished paper for DARPA's Defense Science Office, January 2005.

[59]   See, for example, Shane Mayor et al., "Lidars: A Key Component of Urban Defense," *Biosecurity and Bioterrorism: Biodefense Strategy, Practice, and Science* 6, no. 1 (2008), 45ff; and Barbara McQuiston et al., "Threat Cloud Tactical Intercept and Countermeasure (TACTIC) Program," description in Strategic Technology Office Brochure, 45 (2008).

[60]   While presently prevalent detection systems require manual collection of samples (for example, at daily intervals), the Automated Point Detection System, now in limited use, provides instant indication of a pathogen presence at the detector. These systems might permit real time response and interdiction, especially if they are densely distributed.

[61]   For example, the Federal Bureau of Investigation forensic investigation established that the Amerithrax material was developed using water from the Frederick, MD, water table.

[62]   See, for example, *Planning Guidance for Protection and Recovery Following Radiological Dispersal Device (RDD) and Improvised Nuclear Device (IND) Incidents* (Washington, DC: DHS, 2008).

[63]   Certain biological weapons, particularly many viruses, may have small consequences as contaminants. These may be attractive to some kinds of terrorists precisely because they could function like "neutron bombs," as popularly conceived, leaving buildings and the environment intact, even as they killed people.

after an aerosol attack. Some priority indoor spaces that require clean environments, including hospital rooms, transport hubs,[64] and food processing centers, would similarly need to be assessed, and, before moving outside contaminated areas, vehicles (including airplanes) would require some form of internal and external decontamination.

As terrorists focus on the consequences of biological contamination, they are likely to realize that these effects may induce more disruption, diversion of energies, and economic destruction than more immediate consequences from damage to buildings and infrastructure through explosives and other weapons. This is especially the case with the presently most salient threat, anthrax. A leading analysis concluded that if a kilogram of aerosolized anthrax were dispersed outdoors with reasonable efficiency in Manhattan, it would take more than 40 years to eliminate the resulting contamination.[65]

Biological decontamination is the orphan often left out of the families of thought about WMD. The topic garnered some attention in the wake of the anthrax letter attacks of 2001, when it took 2 years and some $200 million to decontaminate two postal facilities. Techniques have improved with the benefit of that experience, and serious consideration of standards and procedures has begun.[66] But these improvements are not even remotely equal to the challenge at hand. Immediate priority ought to be given to developing standards (at least for anthrax) that are more realistic than the present zero tolerance of contamination, establishing sampling procedures, allocating resources and providing training for sampling teams, and undertaking research and development of improved decontaminants. Not only should efforts on this subject be federally centered, as suggested above, but also they should be internationalized, as Canadian, British, French, Russian, and Asian governments have as much interest as we do in coping with these potential problems; we would profit from their investments in this area. Furthermore, international cooperation would facilitate international trade and environmental controls after an attack on any one of the participating nations.

Among these recommended initiatives, particular stress needs to be placed on the creation of a research and development program for decontaminants. Our present approach overfunds drug development while underfunding decontamination. A few million dollars invested each year by the Homeland Security Science and Technology directorate or the Defense Advanced Research Projects Agency (DARPA)[67] would likely yield much greater benefit than the marginal equivalent

---

[64] DHS usefully charted a pilot project on methods and problems of decontamination of the San Francisco airport after a bioterror attack. See Tina Carlsen et al., "Restoration Plan for Major International Airports After a Bioterrorist Attack" (Livermore, CA: Lawrence Livermore National Laboratory, 2005).

[65] Larry Wein, Yifan Liu, and Terrance J. Leighton, "Evaluation of a HEPA/Vaccine Plan for Indoor Remediation After an Airborne Anthrax Attack," *Emerging Infectious Diseases* 11, no. 1 (January 2005), 71.

[66] The issues were well articulated in the National Research Council's "How Clean is Safe? Reopening Public Facilities After a Biological Attack" (2005). The President's National Science and Technology Council subsequently established a Biological Decontamination Standards Working Group. DHS is developing a guidance document for biological weapons attempting to parallel the "Planning Guidance for Protection and Recovery Following Radiological Dispersal Device (RDD) and Improvised Nuclear Device (IND) Incidents" (2008) cited above.

[67] The Environmental Protection Agency has responsibilities and assets relevant to this problem, but its expertise is more oriented toward superfund and water decontamination than to the problems of urban decontamination after a biological attack.

invested in further drug research. It is particularly imperative that we get this long lead-time work accomplished before an attack.

6. Evolve a theory and practice of citizen self-care.

If, as described above, the demand for health care after a bioterrorist aerosol attack will very probably far exceed the supply of professional services, it follows that many transients and residents of an affected city will be thrown back on their own resources. We experienced aspects of that situation in New Orleans after Hurricane Katrina. But Katrina was much easier to handle than a biological attack would be: the hurricane was largely predicted; as a result, evacuation (reducing the numbers of those affected) and preparation were possible; hurricanes and floods are familiar events and, though the New Orleans experience was extreme, it created well understood needs; the hurricane and related flooding peaked at a recognizable moment; restoration activities were not impeded as they would be if terrorist attacks were repeated, or by the spread of substantial contagion; and, perhaps most significantly, in the weeks after Katrina, the rest of the country was not afraid that it, too, would experience the same disaster, so there was a generous outpouring of support, intake of refugees, and largely unimpeded movement to the damaged city. By contrast, a bioterrorist attack on one city would raise the prospect of attacks on others.[68] These differences all move in the same direction: they reinforce an assessment that citizens of a city stricken by bioterrorist attack will have to rely on their own resources to a degree not known in modern America.

A government that takes consequence management seriously will prepare for this contingency. This challenge has, however, been submerged among other distractions. It is unfamiliar and therefore easily overlooked. When recognized, it is difficult to fit into existing bureaucratic arrangements. More subtly, and more perniciously, it requires the development of a mindset and the allocation of research and support resources away from professionals and their well-established interest groups and toward laymen.

What would a serious program of citizen preparation do? It would:

- prepare messages addressing predictable citizen concerns. These would include, for example, advice about whether to vacuum after an anthrax attack, how to disinfect using common household supplies such as bleach, how to assess symptoms, and so forth. Questions on these topics have to some extent been anticipated by the CDC, among other institutions, but the answers have not been prepared. CDC pleads that it

---

[68] In *Preparing for Catastrophic Bioterrorism*, I recommend that we distinguish between "contained catastrophes" and "comprehensive catastrophes." In contained catastrophes, critical help comes from the outside, as in Katrina and earthquake relief. A comprehensive catastrophe is so extensive that it does not permit one jurisdiction to aid another because "so many jurisdictions are victimized that they are unable to provide resources to one another, [or] jurisdictions are afraid they will be victimized, and so they hoard resources, [or] basic services (particularly fuel, communications and transportation) are so overwhelmed that near-term, external assistance cannot be provided, [or] movement restrictions and transportation system failures prevent rapid external assistance" (19). A significant aerosol anthrax attack on more than one American city (either sequentially or simultaneously) would trigger comprehensive catastrophe. It is possible that one attack alone would have this effect.

would need precise information about the amount, timing, and character of the attack to make such judgments. But information of this kind (for example what strain of anthrax has been released, whether it is antibiotic resistant, when the release occurred) will not be available at the time government authorities announce an attack and trigger these questions. Adequate preparation should include answers developed in calmer circumstances in advance—even though they will be subject to revision as more information becomes available.

- channel a modest, but for these purposes significant, amount of research money (on the order of $20 million per year) into issues relevant to citizen self-care so that the messages described above could be better informed than at present. Our studies of contamination and decontamination have almost exclusively occurred in office and hospital settings and assumed professional equipment, trained and protected workers, and methodical sampling before and after decontamination activity. Serious scientific research about nonprofessional measures will inform those measures.

- build support networks robust and resilient enough to operate in emergencies. As several have suggested, automated systems could permit cellphone users to receive recorded advice after tapping in yes/no responses to standard questions: "Does the patient have a temperature above 101 degrees? Is he or she older than 10 and under 70?" The internet obviously opens broader possibilities. Beyond this, a system of home delivery of water, food, and basic medical supplies could prove invaluable, especially in contaminated areas.

- provide psychological as well as practical support. Messages from government leaders will be important, but they will be counterproductive if they are inconsistent with one another. In our present state of preparation they will be inconsistent. Moreover, studies have repeatedly shown that, when confronted with crisis, laymen look to trusted leaders outside government for advice and for validation of what government leaders are saying. Analysis needs to be done as to who these leaders are likely to be in the wake of biological attack (Family doctors? Local health authorities? Business leaders? Clergymen?), and they need to be integrated into consequence management networks so as to improve the likelihood that their messages will be consistent with those of our governmental leaders. Methods of designating and empowering trusted lay-leaders can also be helpful. Air raid wardens in World War II, for example, appear to have done little of material significance, but had substantial psychological benefits.[69]

7. Develop private partners.

The task of organizing the U.S. Government to address the risks of bioterrorism is critical, extraordinarily complicated and challenging, and immense in its scope. We have, however, seen real progress in this arena since the 9/11 and anthrax letter attacks. Unfortunately, Federal disorganization is only a part of the problem, and even if it were fully addressed, it would leave us

---

[69] Barry Kellman has also pointed out that health insurers would be financially and administratively overwhelmed by high-consequence bioterrorist attacks, and this would compound citizen uncertainties and difficulties.

inadequately positioned. This is because our effort must go further to integrate necessary partners outside the Federal Government. These partners include our state and local governments, our private sector, and foreign governments and enterprises.

The problem of Federal-state-local interaction is described above, and issues of internationalization are discussed below. Alongside these, the challenge of private sector integration must also be met. Intelligence is a case in point. The classic model of intelligence is a system that is tightly held: our government employs technical means (for example, satellites and communications intercepts) and operators (spies) to generate information about threats; this information is passed to government analysts to assess its implications; the resulting understanding is classified, that is, shared only inside the government. This model works reasonably well against states with military assets. Troops and tanks are visible, readily identified, and reasonably limited in number. They can be watched. Expertise about troops and tanks resides largely within governments.

It is plain that this model cannot substantially protect us from bioterrorism. The number of those who can perpetrate bioterrorism is large, and their efforts will be of low visibility. Satellites and other technical means will be largely unhelpful. Human intelligence will be essential, but it must be well informed about laboratory work whose character would be obscure to the typical Central Intelligence Agency agent. We are not only looking for needles in haystacks, but we are also looking for needles that will only be recognized by technically sophisticated observers. The hay straws (instances of innocent biological work) will be in the millions, while trained U.S. operators could at most be in the hundreds (that number would be remarkable). And if an innovative, suspicious activity is discovered, the expertise to assess it is more likely to be in our biotech companies, pharmaceutical companies, medical centers, and academia than in our government.

Our greatest resource for coping with this problem lies in our wealth of commercial and academic talent. Our pharmaceutical salesmen, veterinarians, academics, and others are much more numerous, travel more freely throughout the world, and have more insight than our intelligence agents. Their relationships as mentors, colleagues, and businesspersons are more likely to alert them to suspicious behaviors, unusual requests, and unexpected pathologies. The great diversity of work in our medical centers, universities, biotech enterprises, and pharmaceutical companies also make these the richest sources of analytical insight about activities that have been identified, but not fully comprehended. A 21st-century intelligence enterprise must harness this aspect of America's power if we are to succeed.

Some progress has been made in this respect. A Defense Intelligence Agency panel (the 2020 Group) and a Director of National Intelligence group (the Biological Sciences Evaluation Group) have granted security clearances to a few dozen first-rate experts and convene them regularly to discuss intelligence issues and hypotheses. Some voices have been heard stressing the need for more interaction between the Intelligence Community and the private sector.[70] But bureaucratic,

---

[70] Director of National Intelligence, *Vision 2015: A Globally Networked and Integrated Intelligence Enterprise* (Washington, DC: DNI, n.d.), 13–14, available at <www.dni.gov/Vision_2015.pdf>. See notably the Intelligence Science Board's report, *Integrating Private Sector Information into Intelligence Community Activities*; and Daryl Williams, "Discussion Paper for the December Quarterly ISB Meeting Looking at the Topic: Integrating Private Sector Information into Intelligence Community Activities" (November 2008). The latter paper points out that important intelligence–private sector relationships were developed after the 9/11 attacks, but lost momentum in subsequent years. For example, the Department of Defense's (DOD's) Partnership to Defeat Terrorism (PTDT) is described as "a highly successful global public-private

cultural, and legal barriers[71] inhibit expansion of these beachheads, and we have not yet established an environment in which information and insight is regularly shared so as to establish relationships between those who can contribute across the public-private boundary.

Similarly, our research, development, and production efforts have not yet effectively recognized and integrated the private sector. To be sure, private contractors support DHS, provide the goods for our drug stockpile maintained by HHS, and work on some bioterrorism-related projects with other agencies. Research grants, particularly those awarded by the National Institutes of Health, are a prized source of support to academics and in recent years have become more oriented to the risks posed by bioterrorism. But government procedures, uncertainties about direction, and low payouts have left biotech and pharmaceutical companies largely outside these efforts.

Models exist for improving this situation. During World War II, Merck, the industry leader in pharmaceuticals, supplied personnel to the Federal Government through the simple mechanism of having a reserve unit of its executives. During the Cold War, DOD used Defense Production Act capabilities to establish standby production capacity for critical items that would be needed in an emergency. Similarly, it contracted for the right to conscript civilian aircraft to be used if required for the reinforcement of Europe. The DARPA drug manufacturing project described below has taken a small step in these directions, but policymakers should give them more priority.

Consequence management planning has occurred largely within the government. But our responses to a mass biological attack will be as much driven by private sector enterprises. Our utility, communications, transport, and medical services rely on private no less than public employees. If a city uses postal workers to deliver drugs or establishes points of distribution staffed by clerical workers, why can it not alternatively or additionally use FedEx employees or distribute drugs through pharmacies and at a Wal-Mart?

---

partnering effort that [led through American companies] to relationships with senior leaders in Arab countries, Europe, and the Pacific Rim. From October 2001 to December 2005, an upsurge in patriotism served as a powerful catalyst for the private sector to partner with the USG [U.S. Government]; the PTDT averaged three to four unsolicited requests for partnering per week from leaders occupying senior levels in Fortune 500 companies. Ultimately, the value derived from the private sector leaders was the knowledge that their actions were aiding the U.S. and allies' fight against terrorism. Unfortunately, this eagerness has since been replaced by a medieval city-state mindset that has led private sector entities to create their own intelligence capabilities, build their own operational response units, and institute strategic-level safeguards to protect both their assets and their employees. Discussions with private sector leaders revealed frustration with the perceived lack of action, both post-9/11 and in the present, by U.S. and allied governments. As a result, private sector entities are no longer eager to partner with the USG because the results no longer seem worth the operational risk. Since January 2006, the majority of operational successes in integrating private sector into [Intelligence Community] activities have been based solely on intimate and sensitive trusted relationships" (8).

[71] These occur on both sides of the equation. For example, academics' careers are enhanced by publication, not classified work; businessmen are responsible for generating profit, not ill-paid or unpaid intelligence insight. While physicists and chemists readily accept classification of security relevant aspects of their work and frequently can be found employed in government agencies and national laboratories, many biologists resist this activity. Daryl Williams correctly observes: "The private sector does not trust the USG to protect sensitive information and sources. The USG does not trust the private sector to safeguard classified information" (3).

Private companies also have opportunities and responsibilities with regard to their employees and the public. Buildings can be made safer through better filtration systems, structural adjustments to entries, exits, and windows, paints, and so forth. Enterprises can stock their own drug supplies (relevant to maintaining workforce health and therefore employment in natural epidemics) and provide information and support to employees in the wake of bioterrorist incidents. We have institutionalized expectations about enterprise responsibility for employees in other contexts like for coping with fire and earthquakes. But private enterprise responsibilities for security against terrorism have remained limited to such small steps as establishing check-in stations at the entrance to large buildings.[72]

Though a commission or study group is often an excuse for inaction, such an effort, composed of leaders from business and government and joined by those with biological expertise, could be an important initiative for establishing an agenda for public-private cooperation. The problem of bioterrorism is too large to be solved by government alone.

8. Invest in international approaches to this international problem.

Bioterrorism is an international problem. The pathogens and technologies that enable this mode of terrorism are globally distributed. If a catastrophic act of this kind is perpetrated in this country, it may well be by Americans, just as it was an American who destroyed the Oklahoma City Federal Office Building, and evidently an American who mailed the 2001 anthrax letters. But, as is well recognized, an attack of this kind may also originate abroad, as the 9/11 attacks did. Accordingly, our intelligence and prevention efforts have to be international.

It is less widely perceived that planning for consequence management similarly needs to be international. Whether a bioterrorist attack is conducted domestically or across international borders, and wherever it occurs, its effects will be global. If foot and mouth disease is infiltrated into the United States (an easy thing to do), the havoc that results will be as shaped as much by our trading partners' reactions to American beef as by our own actions. Conversely, a smallpox attack in Moscow will have instantaneous and enormous effects in the United States.[73] And if the consequences of a biological attack in Tokyo or Paris are not well managed, the resulting deaths, disruption, and dissension will attract terrorists to using this weapon against the United States, Israel, and, indeed, all countries. As a result, underpreparation in Tokyo or Paris is almost as serious for the United States as underpreparation here.

---

[72] This is probably a response to lawyers' interpretations of obligations under landlord-tenant law to conform to prevailing security practices.

[73] An anthrax attack in Moscow would have less immediately dramatic effects here, but the effects of contamination (through aircraft passengers and goods shipped from Russia) and travel restrictions would be felt here.

Despite this, America's efforts have been overwhelmingly domestically focused.[74] Our most notable 21st-century intervention on bioterrorism in international fora was to withdraw from negotiations on the Biological Weapons Convention (BWC) Verification Protocol. Without American leadership, there has been limited international collaboration in confronting the problems of bioterrorism.[75] Interpol, the World Health Organization,[76] Group of Seven,[77]and North Atlantic Treaty Organization have an active interest in bioterror issues, but their efforts are constrained by limited budgets and tepid member interest. Bilateral dialogs[78] on terrorism have biological components, but these have rarely led to substantial actions. Among nation-states, only the United

---

[74] "[T]here is a significant disconnect between the thoughtful approach to addressing the challenges [of bioterrorism] domestically and the narrowly framed and inherently limited approach to addressing the same issues internationally as manifested in U.S. funding for international biodefense efforts. This divide between domestic and international approaches, however, signals a failure to recognize the unique and multisectoral nature of biological threats and a lack of imagination in addressing them. Policymakers in the U.S. and around the world need to recognize and understand that biological threats — whether occurring naturally or through deliberate bioterrorist attacks — do not respect borders; they are inherently global in nature. As such, the U.S. response must be equally international in nature." See Marc L. Ostfield, "Strengthening Biodefense Internationally: Illusion and Reality," *Biosecurity and Bioterrorism: Biodefense Strategy, Practice, and Science* 6, no. 3 (2008), 261. Also, "Today, there is no overarching U.S strategy on international biological security. Existing White House biodefense strategies are focused primarily on domestic issues." See "Confronting 21st Century Biological Threats: International Efforts to Strengthen American Biosecurity," unpublished U.S. State Department paper, 1.

[75] There has been more activity with respect to terrorism generally, though it also has suffered from severe limitations. For an overview of United Nations (UN) activity describing particularly the UN Counterterrorism Committee and its expert body, the Counterterrorism Executive Directorate, see Eric Rosand et al., "The UN's Counterterrorism Security Program: What Lies Ahead?" International Peace Academy, October 2007, available at <www.globalct.org/images/content/pdf/reports/unsc_counterterrorism_program.pdf>. These observers offer the following assessment: "Rather than forming part of a comprehensive strategy to address the global terrorist threat . . . each [Security] Council initiative seems to have had an improvisational, *ad hoc* quality. Following each major terrorist attack, often against one of its own members, the Council has reacted with a response that extends well beyond the specific incident at hand, while paying little regard to whether or not it fits into the already existing Council program. In fact, the Council has yet to reflect on its overall effort, where its comparative advantage lies" (6).

[76] The World Health Organization (WHO) and Organization for Economic Co-operation and Development (OECD) are developing the first international pathogen security guidelines, and WHO is administering reporting requirements for disease outbreaks. See WHO, *Revision of the International Health Regulations*, 58th World Health Assembly, Document WHA58.3 (Geneva: WHO, 2005).

[77] The Group of Seven has established a Global Health Security Action Group of ministers and a subordinate group of bioterrorism experts. It has expanded the initiative to include Mexico and the OECD. Stated aims of this effort include cooperation in research, testing, regulating and procuring vaccines and antibiotics; "support the World Health Organization's disease surveillance network and WHO's efforts to develop a coordinated strategy for disease outbreak containment; . . . share emergency preparedness and response plans, including contact lists, and consider joint training and planning; . . . agree on a process for international collaboration on risk assessment and management and a common language for risk communication; . . . improve linkages among laboratories, including level four laboratories, in those countries which have them." See Ministerial Statement, Ottawa (2001), available at <www.ghsi.ca/english/statementottawanov2001.asp>.

[78] And a "Quadrilateral Group" of the United States, Canada, United Kingdom, and Australia.

States and Great Britain have given these issues front-rank attention, and even secondary attention appears to be limited to a handful of countries.[79]

Policymakers should respond to opportunities and imperatives for energizing U.S. leadership and catalyzing international efforts with respect to bioterrorism. An invigoration of discussions about expansion of the BWC will provide a first opportunity for signaling the Obama administration's concerns about bioterrorism. An American international health agenda focused on shared concerns about pandemic risks can build relationships and stimulate activities relevant to bioterrorism risks. Experience with AIDS, SARS, and avian flu, and concerns about the risk of a worldwide influenza pandemic, will heighten receptivity to establishing global disease surveillance programs, common reporting systems, and plans for developing and sharing medical countermeasures. America should immediately enrich international collaboration by expanding the number of HHS attachés now assigned to U.S. Embassies (there are presently 10), supporting international disease surveillance programs, initiating multinational consequence management exercises and response planning,[80] increasing the $26 million annual budget for State Department Biosecurity Engagement Programs,[81] and sustaining DOD investments in laboratory work abroad. Finally, the U.S. Government can support by participating in, and in some instances funding, some private ventures to enhance international cooperation with regard to biosecurity and bioterrorism.[82]

9. Shape the choices of those who might become bioterrorists.

We can reduce the risks of bioterrorism by influencing the perceptions of two constituencies: biologists and terrorists. Our present efforts to shape these perceptions are marginal. Both warrant more attention.

Expertise relevant to bioterrorism is most prevalent, of course, in those who are trained in modern biology, but also in veterinarians, doctors, agricultural specialists, and those in related

---

[79] Russia, Israel, India, and France have some significant activities. The Netherlands, Switzerland, Germany, and Japan are perhaps next in their concern about this risk.

[80] Two exercises, Atlantic Storm and Black ICE (Bioterrorism International Coordination Exercise), have demonstrated the value from this cooperation. See U.S Department of State. *Black ICE (Bioterrorism International Coordination Exercise) After Action Report*, 2006, available at <www.state.gov/documents/organization/79521.pdf>. Additionally, American "TopOff" (Top Officials) annual exercises have begun to involve Canadian and British officials. These efforts, however, have not led to substantial coordinated planning.

[81] The Biosecurity Engagement Program is a geographically expanded, biologically focused offshoot of the Nunn-Lugar Cooperative Threat Reduction program to encourage elimination of WMD programs in the former Soviet Union. (The Nunn-Lugar program began in 1992.) Run through the State Department's Bureau of International Security and Nonproliferation, the Biosecurity Engagement Program offers funding and technical advice to enhance safety and security practices of biological and veterinary labs through training for security personnel, development of personnel reliability systems, and so forth. As important as its concrete achievements, the program develops American relationships with scientists in countries as diverse as Russia, Pakistan, Indonesia, Thailand, Libya, Iraq, and Yemen. A narrower DOD (Defense Threat Reduction Agency) offshoot of the Nunn-Lugar program, the Threat Agent Detection and Response Program, usefully collaborates with several Central Asian countries to secure dangerous pathogens and provide disease surveillance.

[82] For example, the Center for Strategic and International Studies initiated the Global Forum on Biorisks to create a network for information exchange and cooperation on biosecurity projects.

professions. Training need not be at the graduate level. Aum Shinrikyo's sophisticated attempts at biological attacks in the early 1990s were orchestrated by a cult member with less than a year of graduate training in virology. His most relevant knowledge was acquired as an undergraduate veterinarian. However, there is a common characteristic of those likely to provide biological expertise to a terrorist group: it is highly likely that these individuals were trained at one or another institution that was not committed to terrorism. This is very different from most of those who provide bombmaking, kidnapping, and other terrorist expertise. It suggests an opportunity.

Some efforts have been initiated to complement biological educational with ethical discussion, screening, codes of conduct, reporting procedures, and credentialing provisions. We are familiar with such systems for other professionals. For example, the Hippocratic Oath and other ethical concepts are taught early in medical careers, medical schools screen students and will not continue to train and certificate (that is, graduate) those judged to be incompetent or unethical, doctors recognize some obligation to report colleagues who are acting unethically, and professional boards police practitioners. Of course, these systems are highly imperfect. But few would argue that we would be better off without them. No such systems exist, however, for biologists.

In this domain, professional self-regulation is probably better than government regulation. Accordingly, the relevant private sector leaders are the most important actors. Though the role of government is limited, U.S. Government officials can support the domestic and international development of norms and standards for technically proficient biologists and other professionals. Our leaders can provide encouragement and budgetary support to nascent efforts at educational institutions and among American professionals to provide training that sensitizes these professionals to the risks of bioterrorism, indications of misuse, and proper responses when such indications appear. The U.S. Government can support these professional efforts to spread these activities abroad, and the Biosecurity Engagement Program can finance foreign governments and professionals working to the same end.

While the effort to influence biologists aims at keeping them from supporting terrorists, the effort to influence terrorists would aim at keeping them away from biology. Though it may at first seem otherwise, here also moral suasion can be significant. Some terrorists—those who seek to introduce the apocalypse, vandals, or those motivated exclusively by revenge or a search for fame—may only care about reaping destruction. But many others have political motivations and therefore care about the effect of their acts on political constituencies, those who might fund them, and those who represent future recruits. If bioterrorism is seen by these constituencies as severely contrary to their religious or ethical values or to their own power and well-being, it will contribute to deflecting these terrorists from the use of biological weapons.

This opportunity is particularly ripe because an appeal to Islamic constituencies and Islamic values underlies the presently prevalent jihadi terrorism. If delicately and in many cases obliquely provided, our support of religious and ethical condemnation of biological weapons in Islamic fora can yield real benefits. We can also more directly press our moral strength in this area: while we maintain nuclear weapons and employ an unrivaled range of conventional weapons, we have, since 1969, foresworn the development and employment of biological weapons.[83] We can unequivocally campaign against these weapons as associated with crimes against humanity. There

---

[83] Our subscription to the Chemical Warfare Convention in 1997 also put us on record as foreswearing chemical weapons.

is a real chance, as with the dum-dum bullet, that we can make the revulsion from these weapons an effective barrier to their use.

Terrorist reluctance to use biological weapons can also be shaped by both information and disinformation about the ease of developing and employing these weapons and about their likely effects. Though it is commonly said that terrorists cannot be deterred, this conclusion typically results from an excessively limited view of deterrence as something that derives from the threat of retaliation. Deterrence will also be effective if terrorists can be led to conclude that investments in biological weapons will not be worth their costs, either because the costs probably will be high or the likely benefits low, or both.

We can raise perceived costs by flooding relevant Web sites with accounts of difficulty and failure, misleading instructions, fears that initiatives will be detected, and so forth. It is notable that when Aum Shinrikyo abandoned its biological weapons efforts, it was with the conclusion that biological opportunities were red herrings created by the U.S. Government in an attempt to mislead them.[84]

Our smallpox vaccine stockpiles are indicative of how perceptions of lower benefits can diminish the attraction of a biological weapon. A singularly effective campaign to eradicate smallpox in the natural environment made this a difficult pathogen to use as a biological weapon. But the ability for de novo synthesis of this virus will put this possibility back on the table. There is no doubt that even with the ability to vaccinate all 300 million Americans, a smallpox epidemic would kill many both in America and worldwide and would wreak havoc on trade, travel, economies generally, and many other things we value. However, a terrorist who seeks to diminish American power could likely come to recognize that in a world of smallpox American power will be enhanced because our uniquely large vaccine stockpile will relatively protect us, and the possibilities for sharing that stockpile will enhance our power and influence.[85] This recognition will have a deterrent effect.

Policymakers should recognize, in light of these observations, that the "war of ideas" should include influencing not just third party Islamic populations (as at present), but also biologists and terrorists. An inexpensive but robust program directed at influencing biologists and terrorists can yield significant dividends in reducing the likelihood of bioterrorism.

10. Prepare for the unpredictable.

Historically, our security establishment has given great priority to exploiting technological opportunity for our military advantage. Concomitantly, it has aimed to understand how our potential opponents might exploit these technologies. Our goal, as has often been stated, is to avoid technological surprise.

Bioterrorism is unique in the extent to which we will very probably be subject to technical surprise. It has become a cliché to describe aspects of our competitions with terrorists as "asymmetric." By this it is often meant that their offensive opportunities are cheap, easy, and can be selectively pursued, while our protective responsibilities are expensive, difficult, and must

---

[84] This conclusion is drawn from the author's interviews of Aum prisoners in Tokyo, April 2008. Further interviews with these prisoners are ongoing.
[85] Of course, it may be reasoned that possibilities for sharing will introduce tensions in our alliance relationships.

be comprehensively sustained.[86] But the most fundamental asymmetries in coping with the risk of biological terrorism arise from two other characteristics: defensive systems have orders of magnitude longer lead times than the development of biological weapons; and defensive systems (such as vaccine programs, antibiotic developments) are largely observable, while the proliferation and low signature of biological technologies can render offensive work invisible.

In effect, we are competing against terrorists in research, development, and planning, but it is an uneven competition. Studying us, attackers can be expected to perceive and, over time, attempt to circumvent our defenses and exploit our weaknesses. They could do this, for example, by developing antibiotic-resistant strains when we have stockpiled a particular antibiotic, or by circumventing our known means of detection. On the other side of the equation, an attacker's plans are likely to be unpredictable and his preparations hidden. As a consequence, our planning must presume that we will be surprised.

This proposition is more easily stated than assimilated. As an example of how we can be slow to grasp its consequences, I offer the following from my own recent writing:

> With respect to biological attack we are in a position similar to that of Britain in the 1930s, when it confronted the long-range bomber. The bomber—a terror weapon— initially was deemed unstoppable. Indeed, it *was* unstoppable in 1935, when that realization led the British to mount a research and development program to achieve the means to detect and locate aircraft and vector fighters to intercept them. That program produced an effective national air defense system within five years—just in time for the Battle of Britain.

The analogy is, as it was meant to be, suggestive and encouraging. But it is also misleading. Even though it was hard to perceive and develop effective countermeasures, the threat from bombers was predictable and subject to rather precise definition. Systems of defense against bioterrorism must counter a range of pathogens and delivery systems. Worse, that range can now be populated with synthetic creations that combine or mask attributes, and by new creations. Over the years ahead, these offensive capabilities will expand.

Already, the expansion of these capabilities has effectively undermined the previous method of listing a small number of prominent (Class A) and not so prominent (Classes B and C) threats, and then investing in research against them. Recent DHS efforts to make classified "material threat determinations" are more sophisticated.[87] However, they also attempt to pin down a protean threat. They are driven by a presumption that our investments in drug and vaccine

---

[86] In the words of a Roman philosopher, it is easier to inflict a wound than it is to heal it. See Marcus Fabius Quintilianus (Quintilian), *Institutio oratoria*, V, xiii, 3.

[87] The DHS secretary, in consultation with the HHS secretary and the heads of other agencies, as appropriate, is required to assess on an ongoing basis the current and emerging threats posed by chemical, biological, radiological, and nuclear agents and determine which agents present a material threat against the United States sufficient to affect national security (42 USCS § 247d-6b). If DHS determines that a particular agent poses a material threat to the nation, it issues a Material Threat Determination (MTD) for that agent, which then initiates the BioShield process to procure countermeasures against that agent. To date, DHS has issued MTDs for anthrax, botulinum toxin, smallpox, and radiological/nuclear threats. Additional MTDs are in process. See <www.upmc-biosecurity.org/website/focus/agents_diseases/background.html>.

"countermeasures" rest on pathogen-specific responses, that the development of these responses has long lead times (typically on the order of a decade), and therefore that we must predict threats. Acting predominantly through HHS and DOD, our plans call for manufacturing and stockpiling approximately a half-billion doses of drugs and vaccines to cope with smallpox, anthrax, plague, ricin, botulinum, tularemia, brucellosis, and several filoviruses.[88] This is like strengthening the forts along the Maginot Line—a flexible enemy will circumvent our strong points, in this case by using different or idiosyncratically adapted pathogens.

The question is not whether to amend the list; it is how to proceed without being able to create an adequately protective list. Emphasizing the range and unpredictability of risks would change present analyses of alternatives and present preparations. A prime example of this difference, now being gradually grasped, is in our approach to the problems of drug development, production, and stockpiling. The availability of some drug or vaccine treatments is a predicate to all effective consequence management strategies, but that predicate is challenged in a world of unpredictability. How do we cope with that?

The Defense Threat Reduction Agency has begun to emphasize a potential strategy for improving our capabilities to respond to the unexpected by investing research and development funds into broad-spectrum antibiotics and antivirals—drugs whose mechanisms are so fundamental that, instead of targeting pathogen-specific forms of infection, they operate to counter a wide range of threats. A second strategy, which has drawn less attention, is to seek biological paths to boosting, at least temporarily, the immune systems of individuals who may be subject to attack. Both of these strategies warrant investment, but they are extremely difficult to bring to fruition. The magnitude of the difficulty is suggested by the slow and limited success resulting from our substantial sustained research and development to counter natural diseases ranging from the common cold to AIDS to cancer. If broad-spectrum or immune-boosting opportunities were readily realizable, we would long ago have achieved them.

DARPA is exploring a potentially more fruitful path by developing agile, rapidly responsive drug design and manufacturing capabilities. This strategy lies between, on the one hand, our present prediction of specific needs and development and procurement of the identified countermeasures and, on the other hand, trying to develop broad-spectrum, highly general measures. The intermediate strategy supposes that specific pathogen needs cannot confidently be predicted, but that pathogen-specific measures are likely to be the most achievable and effective responses. It concentrates, accordingly, on building a rapid response capability that can design, test, and manufacture countermeasures once a pathogen becomes known, either from intelligence or as a result of an attack. The key ingredients to this response capability are people (drug development and manufacturing experts), drug "scaffolds" that can provide a base for different protein combinations that can be designed to respond to pathogens, manufacturing capabilities that can be immediately devoted to a required task and surged to large volume outputs, and regulatory and budgetary regimes that support, rather than inhibit, these processes.[89]

---

[88] Filoviruses are a subset of a larger class of hemorrhagic fever viruses. The most notorious of the filoviruses are Marburg hemorrhagic fever and Ebola hemorrhagic fever, both of which were produced in quantity in the Soviet biological weapons program.

[89] A Center for Biosecurity paper argues for a public-private partnership that would establish a "multi-product advanced development and production facility" specializing in seven core production technologies. See *Ensuring Biologics Advanced Development and Manufacturing Capability for the United*

This approach is not a panacea and may indeed prove to be less useful than the alternative strategies. It is not easy to engage the relevant resources; agility and speed are more easily promised than achieved; even if achieved, dramatic improvements that accelerate drug development from years to months or even weeks may be too slow to afford effective protection against biological attacks that can be waged repeatedly during the development period and then be modified if a response is developed. But this third strategy warrants investment because it provides a complementary approach that hedges against the failure of the first two strategies. Furthermore, progress in this arena can have large rewards for coping with natural illnesses, as for example the emergence of a lethal variant of the H5N1 virus.

The challenge is not just one of drug development and production. The protean nature of the threat will, over time, undermine or circumvent all rigid defenses. The precept of preparing for the unpredictable should alert concerned policymakers to the need for innovation in all our activities. If the likelihood of surprise were taken seriously, we would, for example, allocate some exercises to examining how we respond to pathogens for which we lack stockpiled drugs or even treatments. Such efforts can be dispiriting for us, and, if not classified (as they should be), they can encourage or guide attackers. But they must realistically be considered and be the subject of our planning.

As another example, our evaluation of points of distribution systems as compared with delivery of drugs by postal workers tends to emphasize speed and efficiency against a single anticipated threat (typically anthrax). But if, as seems to be the case, postal distribution is the more rapid and efficient alternative, how do we value the fact that points of distribution can be used for both vaccination and distribution, while the postal system can only perform the latter function? Perhaps this argues for maintaining two systems, or perhaps we should conclude that sustaining and exercising two standby systems is too difficult and we should choose the more flexible and broadly applicable, even if in some circumstances the less speedy or efficacious, alternative. The policy debate on this point has not crystallized. The wise policymaker will test proposals in this and other contexts by a standard of flexibility.

Similarly, it seems evident that detection systems that are fixed in function and location invite evasion by design. To be sure, counterdetection strategies can be made harder if we classify and obscure detection mechanisms, but novel pathogens or obscure methods and remote places of release are likely to render secrecy a sterile defense. Over the longer term, just as we need an agile drug production system, so also we need an agile detection system. As with the drug production system, security can be achieved either by introducing adaptive capabilities (How quickly and successfully can existing detection systems be modified to account for the appearance of a new pathogen?) or by coupling the system so closely to an adversary's targets that evasion will cause the attack to miss. A research and development program designed to achieve this tight coupling for detection could focus not on aerosol sampling but on sampling of people whose travels or locations

States Government: A Summary of Key Findings and Conclusions (Pittsburgh: University of Pittsburgh Medical Center, Center for Biosecurity, 2008). This study reports a "shared opinion among interviewees... that a facility dedicated to advancing and manufacturing biologic MCMs [medical counter-measures] should have been developed many years ago. This opinion seems to mirror a general belief among the interviewees that the nation is neither adequately nor robustly prepared for the myriad of scenarios and homeland security threats which make conceivable a catastrophic biological attack or infectious disease outbreak" (10).

make them representative of the target set. Such a system might, for example, examine police officers, firefighters, or postal workers whose movements cover a city. Possibly, such a system would use temperature, blood samples, or other indicators measured at the end of shifts to infer whether infection had occurred. A more sophisticated system would examine samples on small biological meters analogous to radiation detection strips.

A system of this kind is obviously futuristic, as is an agile drug production technology. But only if we underwrite and engage in futuristic research of this kind will the future be secure. Offensive capabilities will grow, become more accessible, and become more protean. We will need to be prepared for the unpredictable. Among the many hard problems that policymakers will confront in attempting to cope with the threat of bioterrorism, this will be the hardest.

Conclusion

In the past, great numbers of American men and women suffered heart attacks because they lacked knowledge about their risks and the steps they could take to diminish them. Decades of work developed an understanding of heart disease and clarified measures that could reduce risk: stop smoking, lose weight, control cholesterols, get more exercise, and so forth. A first aim of this paper has been to provide analogous insight into bioterrorism by illuminating both the risks of this catastrophe and the path to risk reduction.

But analysis alone does not keep Americans from dying from heart attacks. For many who read about the risk, an attack seems too remote, the challenges of prevention too difficult or inconvenient, and the benefits too uncertain to warrant the required efforts. Consequently, heart attacks occur more often, and with more severe effects, than if analysis were translated into action. This paper, an analytic product, will be valuable to the extent it stimulates action.

Just as many Americans do not stop smoking or lose weight until after they suffer heart attacks, so we may wait and move vigorously only after we are stricken by catastrophic bioterrorism. If that is the case, this paper will rest on a shelf, possibly to be dusted off and consulted when we are suffering. That will be a sad, if valuable, use of this work: many will have died who could have been saved had we recognized the risks and acted before the attack. The task of analysts is to show the path. The task of leaders is to move along it before the attacks.

www.ingramcontent.com/pod-product-compliance
Lightning Source LLC
Chambersburg PA
CBHW080107010626
45794CB00015B/3297